JESUS
Friend and Savior

JESUS
Friend and Savior

Michael Pennock

AVE MARIA PRESS
Notre Dame, Indiana 46556

Nihil Obstat:
> The Reverend Theodore Marszal, S.T.D.
> Censor

Imprimatur:
> The Most Reverend Anthony M. Pilla, D.D., M.A.
> Bishop of Cleveland

Given at Cleveland, Ohio on 10 November 1989

© 1990 by Ave Maria Press, Notre Dame, IN 46556

International Standard Book Number: 0-87793-420-7

Library of Congress Catalog Card Number: 89-82459

Cover and text design by Katherine Robinson Coleman.

Photography:

Art Resource, N.Y., 142; Byron Broudy, 80; Ron Byers, 182; Ron Carlson, 171; Cleo Freelance Photo, 189; Paul Conklin, 72; Joseph De Caro, 34; Rohn Engh, 154; Robert Escobedo, 133; John E. Fitzgerald, 15, 26, 31, 60, 86, 94, 151; Eugene S. Geissler, 8; Tom Hampson, 62; Brother Patrick Hart (The Peter Watts Way of the Cross, Gethsemani, KY), 130, 144, 163; Donna Jernigan, 21; William Koechling, 39; Jean-Claude Lejeune, 198; Carolyn A. McKeone, 21; Robert Meier, 99; Joanne Meldrum, 161; Patrick Mooney, 36, 100; Steve Moriarty, cover; NASA, 174; Roger W. Neal, 41, 42, 184; Marilyn Nolt, 41, 108; R. Nowitz, 110; Paul A. Pavlik, 59; Gene Plaisted, 69, 77, 123, 166, 192, 194; Religious News Service Photo, 116, 180; Will & Angie Rumpf, 21; James L. Shaffer, 49, 138, 196; Vernon Sigl, 44, 97, 113, 196; Lee Snider, 105, 127, 186; Bob Taylor, 177; Jim Whitmer, 134, 140; Vera Wulf, 52, 53.

Printed and bound in the United States of America.

The Lord presents himself through my students. He has recently shown himself to me in a powerful way through Ken Buccier, a young man whose courageous fight against cancer has inspired me and all of his classmates.

I dedicate this book to Ken, and thank him for being a living sign of Jesus in our midst.

Acknowledgments

I wish to thank my wife, Carol; my inspirational, humble department chairman, Jim Skerl; my colleagues in the theology department of St. Ignatius High School (Cleveland, Ohio); my editors, Diane Houdek and Frank Cunningham, at Ave Maria Press. All of these outstanding people are my friends and have enlivened and encouraged me in their own unique, loving way.

I also wish to thank another friend, colleague and outstanding teacher, Jim Hogan, for writing the Teacher's Manual to this text.

Finally, I want to thank the Lord for all the wonderful students he has sent to me over the years. As my Jesuit friends and mentors have aptly taught me, this book is for God's greater honor and glory.

Contents

chapter 1

Jesus

Who Is This Person?

When Jesus came to the region of Caesarea Philippi he put this question to his disciples, "Who do people say the Son of man is?" And they said, "Some say John the Baptist, some Elijah, and others Jeremiah or one of the prophets." "But you," he said, "who do you say I am?" Then Simon Peter spoke up and said, "You are the Christ, the Son of the Living God."

—Matthew 16:13-16

In This Chapter

We will look at:

- evidence for Jesus' existence
- Jesus and his contemporaries
- Jesus: some modern views

Jesus Christ! These words identify the most significant person in human history. Who is this person Jesus? Peter, Jesus' friend and apostle, answered the question: ". . . the Christ, the Messiah, the Son of God." Peter and all Christians after him identify Jesus as the one Yahweh promised, the savior who came to rescue all people from sin and from death. Anthony de Mello, S.J., told this story about a recent convert. A non-believer questions his friend:

"So you have been converted to Christ?"
"Yes."
"Then you must know a great deal about him. Tell me: What country was he born in?"
"I don't know."
"What was his age when he died?"
"I don't know."
"How many sermons did he preach?"
"I don't know."
"You certainly know very little for a man who claims to be converted to Christ."
"You are right. I am ashamed at how little I know about him. But this much I do know: Three years ago I was a drunkard. I was in debt. My family was falling to pieces. My wife and children would dread my return home each evening. But now I have given up drink; we are out of debt; ours is now a happy home. All this Christ has done for me. This much I know of him"[1]

---

[1] Anthony De Mello, *Song of the Bird* (New York: Image Books, 1984).

9

Oh, dear Lord, three things I pray
To see Thee more clearly
Love Thee more dearly
Follow Thee more nearly
Day by day.

—*Godspell*

Although he did not know a lot of facts about Jesus, this convert really knew Jesus. Jesus touched his life and changed him.

In this book, you will get to know many things about Jesus: his birth and early life, his public ministry, his teaching and miracles, his death and resurrection. You will study what the church teaches about Jesus. You will learn about his path to happiness and discover some of the ways he meets us today. Knowledge *about* Jesus is never enough, though. The secret to understanding Jesus Christ is to experience his love.

Over the coming months, we pray that you may come to know Jesus in your heart as well as in your head.

Who Do You Say I Am?

Please examine your beliefs about Jesus at this stage of your life. Mark the following statements according to this scale:

1 — strongly agree (I really believe this)

2 — agree (I believe this)

3 — don't know (I'm still searching)

4 — disagree (I don't believe this)

_____ 1. Jesus is the Messiah (the Christ), Son of the living God.

_____ 2. Jesus has saved me.

_____ 3. Jesus is love.

_____ 4. Jesus is the Second Person of the Blessed Trinity.

_____ 5. Jesus is *the* person for others.

_____ 6. Jesus lives.

_____ 7. Jesus is my friend.

_____ 8. Jesus has conquered sin and death.

_____ 9. Jesus can be found today in the church, sacraments, scripture and personal prayer.

_____ 10. Jesus *loves* me.

. discuss .

What do you think each of these statements means?

Did Jesus Exist?

Jesus of Nazareth lived in Palestine nearly 2,000 years ago. The whole Christian religion rests on this person — his life, his death, his resurrection. The entire New Testament testifies to the meaning of Jesus. The gospels especially take up Jesus' public ministry: his teaching, his miracles and his passion, death and resurrection.

The gospels are expressions of faith, however, not neutral documents compiled by objective observers. New Testament writings were composed by believers, that is, those who accept that Jesus is the Christ, the Lord and Savior of the universe.

A good question to ask is whether any evidence for the historical Jesus exists outside of the New Testament. Palestine was a minor though bothersome province in the vast Roman Empire. But some Romans noticed the existence of Jesus through the actions of his followers, known as Christians, who claimed that this Jesus, put to death by the Roman prefect, Pontius Pilate, still lived. Their message, guided by the Holy Spirit, spread like wildfire across the Roman Empire. Three Roman writers — Suetonius, Tacitus and Pliny the Younger — mentioned Jesus or his followers.

Roman Sources. In the early part of the second century, the Roman author Suetonius compiled biographies of the first 12 Roman emperors, from Julius Caesar onward. In *Life of Claudius* he says of the emperor:

> He expelled the Jews from Rome on account of the riots in which they were constantly indulging, at the instigation of Chrestus (Christ).[2]

Suetonius, in his retelling of the Jewish expulsion from Rome in A.D. 49, assumed that Jesus was there. Most likely, when early Christian missionaries went to syn-

. journal .

Write a short paragraph in your journal describing where you are right now in your relationship to Jesus. Then write another paragraph describing where you would like to be when you finish this book.

---

[2] Suetonius, *Claudius* 25.4 as cited by F.F. Bruce in *Jesus and Christian Origins Outside the New Testament* (Grand Rapids, Michigan: William B. Eerdmans Publishing Company, 1974), p. 21.

agogues in Rome to tell the Jews that their long-awaited
Messiah had come, they met with such resistance that
street riots resulted. Claudius believed that Christians and
Jews were members of the same religious sect. He banished
them both because of the civil disturbance that resulted
from their infighting. Luke writes that when Paul arrived
in Corinth around A.D. 50,

> he met a Jew called Aquila whose family came from
> Pontus. He and his wife Priscilla had recently left Italy
> because an edict of Claudius had expelled all the Jews
> from Rome (Acts 18:2).

In his *Annals*, the Roman historian Tacitus writes of the
great fire that swept through Rome in A.D. 64. The
Emperor Nero (stepson and successor to Claudius) probably was responsible for the fire and, to calm the anger of
the Roman citizens against him, blamed the Christians. He
burned many Christians and exposed others to wild beasts.
Tacitus, writing in A.D. 115-117, recounts the story of the
fire and Nero's successful attempt to blame the Christians:

> They got their name from Christ, who was executed
> by sentence of the procurator Pontius Pilate in the
> reign of Tiberius. That checked the pernicious super-
> stition for a short time, but it broke out afresh—not
> only in Judaea, where the plague first arose, but in
> Rome itself, where all the horrible and shameful things
> in the world collect and find a home.[3]

Tacitus went out of his way to seek information about
the origins of Christianity. Perhaps he checked official
Roman records—possibly including Pontius Pilate's reports to Rome. Significantly, this is the only mention of
Pilate in all ancient Roman histories, though the Jewish
writers Philo and Josephus record his cruel rule in Judea.

Pliny the Younger was a master letter writer. In A.D. 111
he was appointed imperial legate of the Roman province of
Bithynia in northwest Asia Minor. He often wrote to the
Roman emperor Trajan. In one letter he asked the emperor

---

[3] Tacitus, *Annals* 15.44 as cited by Donald Senior, C.P., in *Jesus: A Gospel Portrait*
(Dayton: Pflaum, 1975), pp. 10-11.

how he should treat the ever-growing religious group known as the Christians.

Pliny's letter and Trajan's reply are too lengthy to quote, but here are some interesting points. 1) Pliny mentioned that the "superstition" of Christianity had spread so rapidly that the pagan temples had fallen into disuse. Those who sold sacrificial animals were in serious economic trouble. 2) Pliny told the emperor that he freed Christians who rejected Christ and agreed to worship the pagan gods and the emperor, but that he condemned to death Christians who persisted in their beliefs about Jesus Christ. 3) Pliny recounted the Christian custom of celebrating the Eucharist on "a fixed day of the week."

Trajan's letter of response told Pliny that he had acted well in relation to the Bithynian Christians. He wrote that Pliny should punish any believing Christians who came to his attention, but also said that Pliny should not go looking for them. Trajan saw the Christians as potentially dangerous, but not so much of a threat that they had to be hunted down like criminals.

We can conclude by saying that the Roman historians do not have much to say about Jesus, but they do assume that he actually existed.

Jewish Sources.   An interesting reference to Jesus comes from the colorful Jewish historian Josephus. Born around A.D. 37, Josephus commanded the Jewish forces in Galilee during the revolt of A.D. 66-70. The Romans captured him, but because he predicted that the commander-in-chief of the Romans in Palestine, Vespasian, would one day be emperor, his life was spared. Vespasian did become emperor in A.D. 69, and Josephus became his friend.

Josephus composed a 20-volume history of the Jews, the *Jewish Antiquities*, to demonstrate to the Romans and to the Jew-hating emperor Domitian (A.D. 81-96) that the Jews were a noble people. In the 18th book he mentioned John the Baptist, calling him a good man. In the 20th book he noted that Annas the Younger — the son of the high priest mentioned in the gospels—put to death James the Just (in A.D. 62), the leader of the Christian community in Jerusalem.

Of most interest to us, however, is Josephus' account of the troubles the Jews suffered under the governorship of Pontius Pilate (A.D. 26-36):

> Now about this time lived Jesus, a wise man, if indeed he should be called a man. He was a doer of wonderful works, a teacher of men who receive the truth with pleasure, and won over many Jews and Greeks. He was the Christ. And when Pilate, at the information of the leading men among us, sentenced him to the cross, those who loved him at the start did not cease to do so, for he appeared to them alive again on the third day as had been foretold—both this and ten thousand other wonderful things concerning him—by the divine prophets. Nor is the tribe of Christians, so named after him, extinct to this day.[4]

Scholars don't believe this passage comes entirely from Josephus because it sounds as though a believer wrote it. They theorize that certain passages that support Christian belief were added later by a Christian copyist. Examples of this are the phrase, "if indeed he should be called a man," and references to Jesus as the Christ (Messiah) and his resurrection. The significant point for our purpose, however, is that Josephus did not question the actual historical existence of Jesus.

Another reference to Jesus occurs in the Babylonian Talmud, a commentary on Jewish law written in the third century after Christ. This passage mentions a certain Yeshu (Jesus) who practiced magic and led Israel away from true Jewish worship. It also reports that this man had disciples and was "hanged on the eve of Passover."

▪ discuss ▪

1. Does the scarcity of references to Jesus in Roman and Jewish material pose a problem for believers? Why or why not?
2. Does the evidence presented above make it easier for you to accept the historical Jesus? Why or why not?

---

[4] Josephus, *Jewish Antiquities*, Vol. 18, as cited by Nahum N. Glazer in *Jerusalem and Rome: The Writings of Josephus* (New York; Meridian Books, Inc., 1960), p. 145.

3. As a class, list some reasons why it is important that Jesus really existed.

Jesus and His Contemporaries

What did people who rubbed shoulders with Jesus in his own lifetime on this earth think of him? Who was this man?

The gospels are our main source of knowledge about Jesus. They contain interesting insights about how his contemporaries accepted or rejected him.

John the Baptist.   Scripture tells us that John the Baptist was the son of Elizabeth, Mary's cousin. He probably grew up some distance from Jesus' own small village of Nazareth in Galilee. One tradition says John may have been raised in the desert near the Dead Sea in Judea by a monastic community known as the Essenes.

As a young man, John received a call from God to prepare the way for the Messiah. He preached a message of reform and baptized people as a sign of their readiness to accept the Messiah when he would come.

When the people ask John if he is the Messiah, he tells them:

> "I baptize you in water for repentance, but the one who comes after me is more powerful than I, and I am not fit to carry his sandals; he will baptize you with the Holy Spirit and fire" (Mt 3: 11).

When Jesus approaches him for baptism, John says, "It is I who need baptism from you, and yet you come to me" (Mt 3:14). He recognizes Jesus as the one whose coming he has anticipated.

But after Herod Antipas arrested the Baptist, John heard in prison of Jesus' wonderful deeds and words and it was no longer entirely clear to him that Jesus was the Promised One.

> Now John had heard in prison what Christ was doing and he sent his disciples to ask him, "Are you the one who is to come, or are we to expect someone else?" (Mt 11:2-3).

Jesus may not have been the kind of Messiah John the Baptist was expecting.

In John's gospel, however, written later than the others, John the Baptist clearly announces Jesus as the savior:

> "Look, there is the lamb of God that takes away the
> sin of the world" (Jn 1:29).

Jesus' Family and Neighbors.   You would think that those who knew Jesus best would be his biggest admirers. Unfortunately, this was not the case. Jesus began his ministry in Galilee, the northern region of Israel. He taught wonderful things and performed many miracles there. After a while, he returned to preach the good news in his home town of Nazareth:

> Leaving that district, he went to his home town, and
> his disciples accompanied him. With the coming of the
> Sabbath he began teaching in the synagogue, and most
> of them were astonished when they heard him. They
> said, "Where did the man get all this? What is this
> wisdom that has been granted him, and these miracles
> that are worked through him? This is the carpenter,
> surely, the son of Mary, the brother of James and Joset
> and Jude and Simon? His sisters, too, are they not here
> with us?" And they would not accept him (Mk 6:1-4).

Jesus was so ordinary that his neighbors simply could not believe he was special. "Why he is just the village carpenter. How could God be speaking through him?" They simply rejected him.

How did Jesus react? Mark's gospel tells us that Jesus observed quite wisely, "A prophet is despised only in his own country, among his own relations and in his own house" (Mk 6:4). He also tells us that Jesus:

> . . . could work no miracle there, except that he cured
> a few sick people by laying his hands on them. He was
> amazed at their lack of faith (Mk 6:5-6).

On another occasion, Jesus went home and such a crowd gathered around him that it was impossible even to eat a meal.

When his relations heard of this, they set out to take charge of him; they said, "He is out of his mind" (Mk 3:21).

Jesus' own people not only did not believe in him, they thought he was crazy!

Jesus and His Townsfolk

Please read Luke 4:14-30. Answer the following questions.

1. What was being proclaimed in the passage Jesus was reading?

2. What did Jesus say to anger his fellow citizens?

3. What surprising thing did the people try to do to Jesus?

> He came to Nazareth where he had been brought up, and went into the synagogue on the Sabbath day as he usually did.
>
> —Luke 4:14

The Pharisees. The Pharisees were the most important religious group of Jesus' day. Their name means "separated ones." They wanted to separate themselves from non-Jews and from Jews who refused to live the Law. Many *scribes*, men trained in law, were members of the Pharisees. Their oral traditions were added to the Law. These traditions gave detailed regulations about the Sabbath observance, ceremonial washings, and tithing, that is, donating a set amount of their money and goods for religious purposes.

The Pharisees had good intentions. They thought that if they lived the Law God gave to the Hebrew people very strictly, then God would have mercy and send the Messiah. This was a worthy goal, but their rules and regulations burdened the average person with needless guilt and worry.

Many Pharisees objected to Jesus and his message because Jesus appealed to people's hearts and the spirit of love rather than to strict observance of the Law. Some Pharisees were jealous of the influence Jesus had over the people.

The Pharisees saw Jesus as a formidable opponent; they recognized him as an important teacher who influenced people. They saw him as a threat to their own position of authority over people.

Two Pharisees

1. Please read Luke 7:36-50 and answer the following questions.

    a. What was this Pharisee's name?

    b. What common courtesies did he fail to extend to Jesus?

    c. How does Jesus defend his actions?

    d. What are the people wondering about Jesus?

2. Please read Acts 5:34-39.

    Gamaliel, a Pharisee and a member of the Jewish governing body—the Sanhedrin—had an open mind concerning the early followers of Jesus, the Christians.

    In your own words, what was Gamaliel's advice to his fellow countrymen?

Discuss some examples of how Gamaliel's advice might apply in our day.

The People.   Finally, we turn to the common people Jesus met in his ministry. What did they think of Jesus? Turn again to the quote given at the beginning of this chapter. There you will see that many thought Jesus was John the Baptist, Elijah or Jeremiah come back to life, or some other great prophet. Listen to what some said on Palm Sunday:

> And when he entered Jerusalem, the whole city was in turmoil as people asked, "Who is this?" and the crowds answered, "This is the prophet Jesus from Nazareth in Galilee" (Mt 21:10-11).

Some even proclaimed when he rode into Jerusalem on a donkey:

Blessed is he who is coming
as King *in the name of the Lord!* (Lk 19:38).

Certainly many people who heard Jesus thought of him as a wonder-worker and an impressive preacher. Many people also experienced his love and compassion and knew he was a good person. However, not everyone believed. Perhaps the majority had a "wait and see" attitude. Jesus was special, but who was he really? Many people, including his closest friends, abandoned him when he was arrested and condemned to death.

Pontius Pilate.   A central figure in Jesus' last hours, Pontius Pilate was the fifth Roman procurator who governed the provinces of Idumea, Judea and Samaria from A.D. 26-36. Since Jerusalem is in Judea, he was the authority in charge at the time of Jesus' arrest.

When the Jewish leaders brought Jesus to Pilate, he questioned Jesus by asking if he were the king of the Jews. If Jesus claimed to be king, he would be guilty of sedition under Roman law, a crime punishable by death. Jesus answered Pilate:

"Mine is not a kingdom of this world; if my kingdom were of this world, my men would have fought to prevent my being surrendered to the Jews. As it is, my kingdom does not belong here" (Jn 18:36).

Pilate saw Jesus as an innocent man, certainly not a threat to the emperor's authority. However, his will was weak; he gave in to pressure and had Jesus crucified.

Other Views of Jesus

Caiaphas: Read Matthew 26:57-68.
Who was he?

What did he want to know about Jesus?

Herod Antipas: Read Mark 6:14-16.
Who does Herod think Jesus is?

God: Read Matthew 3:16-17 and Matthew 17:1-8.
What does God reveal about Jesus?

What are the two events in which this revelation takes place?

Jesus: Some Modern Views

Who do people today think Jesus is? Some people pay little attention to Jesus. One writer observed that if Jesus came today people wouldn't crucify him. They would merely invite him to dinner, hear what he had to say, and then make fun of it. Other people have a negative view of Jesus. They believe Jesus taught a faulty message that has thwarted humanity's development.

Jesus and his values, however, are very much alive in our world today. Countless millions see in Jesus the perfect model for our lives. They accept him as the Lord who has saved them and who brings meaning to their own existence. Here are some of today's answers to Jesus' question "Who do people say that I am?"

Jesus: Person for Others.   We all want to be happy. We all want to satisfy the hunger of our restless hearts. We all want to be understood and accepted. Christians believe that Jesus shows the way to happiness. His life and his message proclaim that when you give yourself in love you will find true joy. When you love you will experience what life is all about. You will find peace.

When you are *for others* you discover that everyone is your brother and sister. This truth shows you that you are not alone. Your restless heart is made for love, a love you can find in serving others.

Jesus: The Savior.   Christians recognize in Jesus a personal savior, a living person who contacts them in prayer, in scripture, in the sacraments and through the church. As savior, Jesus heals the sickness of sin and helps us overcome our evil ways. He has won for us eternal life by virtue of his sacrifice on the cross. Jesus continues to work wonders by giving people courage and strength to live their lives daily in a spirit of love.

Ask people if Jesus has ever helped them. You'll be surprised at how many credit Jesus with saving them from an empty life.

Jesus: Way to Freedom.   In many places around the world, millions of suffering people are victims of political, social and economic oppression. Starvation claims thousands of lives daily. Millions of people can't worship God the way they want to or to express themselves freely. More than half the world lives under dictatorships that crunch the human spirit. To many of these suffering people, Jesus means freedom.

Jesus preached the good news that God's kingdom has arrived. Jesus lives in the hearts of his followers. He commands his followers to work for everyone's freedom from hunger and from every other kind of oppression.

Jesus himself asks if we see him . . .

In the inner-city infant crying with hunger pangs:

"I was hungry and you gave me food."

In the rebellious teenager thirsting
for love and understanding:

"I was thirsty and you gave me drink."

In the lonely classmate searching for a friend:

"I was a stranger and you made me welcome."

In the street person in ragged clothes:

"I was lacking clothes and you clothed me."

In the AIDS victim shunned by neighbors and friends:

"I was sick and you visited me."

In the desperate face of a lonely prisoner:

"I was in prison and you came to see me."

Jesus: The Human Face of God.   Many people believe that Jesus is God's Son who became human. They look to him for answers to our most basic questions: "Why am I here?

Where am I going? What is a good life? What does it mean to be human?"

Jesus is the clue to figuring out the universe. He is Lord of the world—the one person who can command and deserves our utmost loyalty. By looking at Jesus' life and teaching, we will discover what it means to be really human. Jesus is *the* model for all of us to follow.

What about you? Who do you say Jesus is? As you study Jesus in this book and meet him in the New Testament, in prayer and in your Christian brothers and sisters, may he help you discover an answer to this question.

▪ *journal* ▪

Interview one peer and two adults on who they think Jesus is.

Write up your findings in your journal. Discuss how their views are similar to or different than yours. Be prepared to share in class.

▪ *discuss* ▪

Read together Matthew 25:31-46. As a class come up with a list of people in your school and families who might be hungry, thirsty, sick, or impoverished in some way.

Brainstorm some concrete things you can do to respond to the needs of each of these people.

▪ *summary* ▪

1. Jesus asked his disciples and he asks us today: "Who do you say that I am?"

2. The New Testament is our primary source of information about the existence of Jesus.

3. Limited evidence outside the New Testament refers to the existence of Jesus. These Roman and Jewish writers either allude to him or mention his followers: Suetonius, Tacitus, Pliny the Younger, Josephus and the Babylonian Talmud.

4. Jesus' contemporaries had many different views on who he was. Some recognized him as a great prophet or the king of the Jews. Others thought he was a misguided, harmless teacher. John the Baptist called Jesus the lamb of God. Some of Jesus' relatives and neighbors thought he was crazy.

5. The Pharisees, a pious group of laymen and scribes, saw Jesus as a threat to their influence over the people. Jesus won people's hearts by appealing to love, in contrast to the Pharisees' strict observance of the Law.

6. Views of Jesus held by people today include:

    a. Jesus is the perfect model of service, a person for others.

    b. Jesus has come to rescue us from sin and death; he is the savior of humanity.

    c. Jesus and his message liberate us from oppression; he is the way to freedom.

    d. Jesus is the perfect human—God's own Son—the human face of God. He shows us how to live happy, meaningful, loving lives.

▪ *focus questions* ▪

1. Identify each of the following Roman authors and briefly discuss what they wrote concerning Jesus' historical existence: Suetonius, Tacitus, Pliny the Younger.

2. Who is Josephus and what did he say about Jesus? Why is his testimony considered unreliable?

3. Identify each of the following and tell what they thought of Jesus: John the Baptist, Jesus' neighbors and relatives, Peter, Pontius Pilate.

4. Where did Jesus begin his public ministry?

5. Who were the Pharisees and what did they believe? Why was Jesus a threat to them?

6. Briefly explain each of the following contemporary images of Jesus:

        Person for Others   Way to Freedom
        Savior   Human Face of God

▪ *journal entries* ▪

1. Write a personal letter to Jesus telling him two things:

    a. Who you are. Mention your strengths and gifts. Tell him what is going on in your life right now.

    b. What you think of him. In personal terms, answer Jesus' question, "Who do you say that I am?"

2. *Enriching your vocabulary.* Using a good dictionary, look up the meaning of the following words. Write the definitions in your journal.

acronym	formidable	panoramic
contemporary	instigate	pernicious
fabricate	obscure	sedition

Prayer Reflection

At the Last Supper, Jesus prayed for all of his followers. His powerful prayer reminds us that he will never leave us. He has tremendous things in store for us. Reflect joyfully on this prayer:

Father,
I want those you have given me
to be with me where I am,
so that they may always see my glory
which you have given me
because you loved me
before the foundation of the world.
Father, Upright One,
the world has not known you,
but I have known you,
and these have known
that you have sent me.
I have made your name known to them
and will continue to make it known,
so that the love with which you loved me may be in
    them,
and so that I may be in them.

—John 17:24-26

▪ *reflection* ▪

Jesus wants to love you! Think about that. He wants to live in your heart.

▪ *resolution* ▪

Jesus wants to be your friend. Put yourself in the Lord's presence and ask yourself each day of this coming week, "Do I want to be the Lord's friend? And if so, how can I love him better?" Listen carefully to the insights the Lord will send to you.

chapter 2
Jesus
The Early Years

She will give birth to a son and you must name him Jesus, because he is the one who is to save his people from their sins.

—Matthew 1:21

In This Chapter

We will look at:

- the infancy narratives
- the childhood and youth of Jesus

The American short story writer O. Henry wrote a masterpiece entitled "The Gift of the Magi," the story of a young married couple—Della and Jim.[1] Like many couples starting their lives together, they were poor and had little extra cash. In fact, they could not afford to buy each other a Christmas present. But they were very much in love.

Della desperately wanted to buy Jim a chain for his heirloom pocket watch. She had an idea. Her beautiful long hair was the envy of every woman she met. On the day before Christmas, she decided to cut her hair and sell it to the wigmaker for the money to buy Jim his Christmas present.

Jim got home from work late that cold Christmas eve. When he saw Della his mouth dropped open. She looked so different.

> "Jim, darling," she cried, "don't look at me that way. I had my hair cut off and sold it because I couldn't have lived through Christmas without giving you a present. It'll grow out again—you won't mind, will you?"

Jim embraced his wife and then presented his own Christmas gift to her—a pair of valuable combs for her hair. Della had admired these combs for a long time; they were now worthless until her hair grew in once again.

Della told Jim not to worry and happily gave him the gift she had gotten for him. When he opened it, he simply smiled.

---

[1] From *The Complete Works of O. Henry* (Garden City, New York: Doubleday, Doran & Company, Inc., 1936).

"Let's put our Christmas presents away and keep 'em
a while. They're too nice to use just at present. I sold
the watch to get the money to buy your combs."

O. Henry's story conveys the real spirit of Christmas.
Jim and Della sacrificed their most precious possessions to
make each other happy. Their gifts represented themselves. In giving away all they had for the other, they found
the true meaning of love, the meaning of Christmas.

Christmas is about gift-giving. The story of Jesus' birth
does more than merely chronicle the birth of a baby some
2,000 years ago. It shouts across the centuries the powerful
message that God loves us! God's love, care and concern
is so wonderful that Jesus is God's eternal gift to us.

You Are Gift!

Reflect on all you are as a person, all that God has given
to you. In the spaces provided on the personal banner
opposite, respond to the questions below. Use symbols for
spaces 2 and 3 and words for the rest.

Write a personal motto that guides your life (1).

For spaces 2 and 3, please create two symbols that represent
God's greatest gifts to you.

Write a sentence to describe what is most special about
you (4).

Who are the three most important people God has sent to
you in your life (5)?

Use a word to describe what these people have meant for
you (6). (For example, mother—life).

What three talents has God given you that make you
special (7)?

. *journal* .

Compose a short prayer of thanksgiving to God for all he has given to
you as a person.

. *discuss* .

Show your personal banner to a classmate. Discuss your
personal mottoes and how they are gifts.

1

2 3

4

5

6

7

The Infancy Narratives

No one recorded the details of the birth of Jesus. Only Matthew and Luke mention it at all, and they have very different perspectives. How reliable are their accounts?

Most scholars acknowledge that the gospels relate religious truth. Each gospel writer proclaimed the good news of salvation in a unique way. Matthew and Luke include stories of Jesus' early years primarily to show that the risen Jesus, Lord of the universe, was special from the very beginning of his life on earth. Historical detail surrounding his early years was not as important to them as the theological significance.

Keeping this in mind, let us nevertheless turn to the nativity stories to see what they tell us about Jesus. We will examine what, when, where, who, how and why.

What?   We cannot state with total accuracy what is historical, prophetical or theological in the early chapters of Luke and Matthew. Take, for example, Matthew and Luke's versions of Jesus' family tree. These genealogies might not give an accurate historical record of Jesus' ancestors, but they do tell us *what* is taking place in the birth of Jesus.

Scripture scholars conclude that Matthew's and Luke's genealogies are primarily *theological.* They hint at Jesus' true identity—he is both the Son of God and a human being like us. Luke's version traces Jesus all the way to Adam and then to God. Luke is writing for a *Gentile*-Christian (that is, non-Jewish) audience. For Luke, Jesus is the savior of *all* people, both Gentile and Jew alike. Thus, he traces Jesus to Adam, the father of everyone. Luke goes on to say that Jesus is also the Son of God. His genealogy reveals two important truths: Jesus is both God and human.

Matthew begins with Jesus' ancestors and moves forward to Jesus. Scholars have shown that Matthew wrote his gospel for *Jewish*-Christians. Matthew's readers were familiar with Old Testament prophecy. So, Matthew begins with the father of the Jewish people, Abraham, and with Israel's greatest king, David, to stress Jesus' identity as the Messiah promised by Yahweh long ago. The birth of Jesus means that God fulfills the promises he made to his Chosen People.

What is important about Jesus' birth?
Read Matthew 1:1-17 and
Luke 3:23-38
the ancestry of Jesus

When?   Matthew tells us that Jesus was conceived and born during the reign of King Herod the Great. Luke tells us that John the Baptist and Jesus were both conceived during Herod's reign.

Herod the Great was from Idumea. A half-Jew, he accepted Greek customs and practices. Herod was a friend of the Roman emperor, Caesar Augustus, who allowed him to rule Palestine. He was politically smart and intellectually and physically vigorous. He was also a cruel, vindictive ruler. Through ruthless but effective methods, he had become king in Palestine. He killed his eldest sons for fear that they might usurp his throne. The story of the Slaughter of the Holy Innocents at the time of Jesus' birth (cf. Mt 2: 16-18) would have fit his character perfectly. The Jews despised Herod. His pagan practices and cruel, bloodthirsty rule alienated his subjects.

Most scholars agree that Jesus was born before 4 B.C., the year Herod the Great died. A common range of years is 8-6 B.C. In addition, Luke writes:

> Now it happened that at this time Caesar Augustus issued a decree that a census should be made of the whole inhabited world. This census—the first—took place while Quirinius was governor of Syria, and everyone went to be registered, each to his own town (Lk 2:1-3).

Based on the authority of the Jewish historian Josephus, many scholars date Quirinius' census at A.D. 6. *The Jerusalem Bible* explains that this census probably began in Palestine as early as 8-6 B.C. as part of a general census of the Empire. This general census would have taken many years, perhaps only concluding in A.D. 6 under Quirinius.

Where?   Matthew tells the story of the Magi visiting Jesus from the east:

> After Jesus had been born at Bethlehem in Judaea during the reign of King Herod, suddenly some wise men came to Jerusalem from the east asking, ''Where is the infant king of the Jews? We saw his star as it rose and have come to do him homage'' (Mt 2:1-2).

Where and when was Jesus born?

Read Matthew 2:1-23
the visit of the magi
and the flight into Egypt
and Luke 2:1-20
the birth of Jesus

Matthew wants to show that Jesus is a king, someone deserving of our loyalty and worship.

The term *magi* probably refers to astrologers from the east, perhaps from Persia, Babylon or the Arabian deserts. They were Gentiles, or non-Jews. Matthew tells the story of the magi to show that Gentiles embrace Jesus as the Messiah while Jews don't recognize him.

Gift Giving

The story of the Magi's gift-giving is richly symbolic.

> **Gold** is a gift worthy of a king.
>
> **Incense** is a gift burnt in offering to God.
>
> **Myrrh** is an ointment used to prepare a body for burial—it testifies to the suffering the Son of Man would endure.

These three gifts make an important statement: *Jesus is truly the King of the universe, the Son of God who will undergo suffering for his people.*

Think of three gifts you can give to the Lord right now. Think about and respond to the following.

Gold: What is your best quality?

How can you put it at God's service?

Incense: What bad habit should you let go of as a sacrifice to the Lord?

Myrrh: What is your greatest hardship that you can offer to God in thanksgiving for all he has done for you?

In contrast to Matthew's story of important royal visitors from the east, Luke relates the story of poor shepherds:

> Now it happened that when the angels had gone from them into heaven, the shepherds said to one another, "Let us go to Bethlehem and see this event which the Lord has made known to us." So they hurried away and found Mary and Joseph, and the baby lying in the manger (Lk 2:15-16).

In Luke's gospel, in contrast to Matthew's, humble people like the shepherds recognize Jesus' true identity. Because these shepherds roamed the hillsides away from the Temple and synagogues, their countrymen often accused them of not observing all the Jewish laws. In Luke's gospel, Jesus compassionately reaches out to the poor, the outcasts, the sinners.

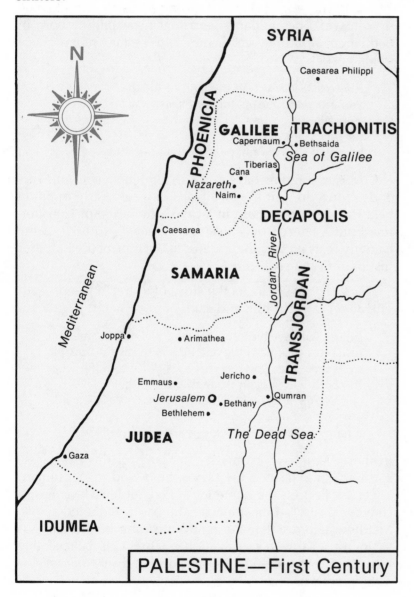

PALESTINE—First Century

Matthew and Luke tell different stories but they agree that Jesus was born in Bethlehem, a small village only six miles southwest of Jerusalem. In the Old Testament, Ruth, Jesse and David are associated with Bethlehem. Ruth, a symbol of great faith, is a key ancestor of David. Jesse, David's father, made his home in Bethlehem. And it is in Bethlehem that Samuel anointed David king of Israel (1 Sm 16:1-13). The Jews believed that the Messiah would come from David's descendants, and that he would be born in Bethlehem. Matthew echoes an Old Testament prophecy in his gospel:

And you, Bethlehem, in the land of Judah,
you are by no means the *least among the leaders of
 Judah,*
for *from you will come a leader*
who will *shepherd* my people Israel (Mt 2:6).

Christian pilgrims have gone to Bethlehem since the second century to visit the birthplace of Jesus. Early tradition held that Jesus was born in a cave. The Emperor Constantine built a church over this cave. Today's Church of the Nativity rests on this site; it dates to the time of the Emperor Justinian in the sixth century.

Who? Matthew tells us the story of a dream Joseph had. The angel came to him and said:

[Mary] will give birth to a son and you must name him Jesus, because he is the one who is to save his people from their sins. Now all this took place to fulfill what the Lord had spoken through the prophet:
 *Look! the virgin is with child and will give birth to a
 son whom they will call Immanuel,*
a name which means "God-is-with-us" (Mt 1:21-23).

In these verses we learn why the birth of this baby is so earth-shaking: Jesus is the savior; he is God-made-human.

Let's reflect on the name *Jesus.* Like all Jewish names, it conveys profound meaning. In the passage quoted above, Matthew tells us that the literal meaning of the name is savior or "Yahweh is salvation." Christians believe that Jesus is indeed the savior of the world and also *Immanuel* — God-is-with-us.

Jesus was a common name in our Lord's day; it was a late form of the Hebrew name Joshua (Yehoshua). Jesus' last name (surname) was *not* Christ. *Christ* is a title that means "Messiah" or "Anointed One." To distinguish our Lord from others who bore the same first name, one of the following would have been used:

- *Jesus from Nazareth* or *Jesus the Nazarene.* People were sometimes identified by their hometown.

- *Jesus the Carpenter.* People often took the name of their professions. Mark's gospel informs us that Jesus worked as a carpenter before he began to preach.

- Finally, Jesus was known as *Jesus, son of Joseph* or, in the Aramaic/Hebrew, *Jesus bar (ben) Joseph* (for example, Jn 1:45).

How? Both Luke and Matthew agree that Jesus was born of the *virgin,* Mary. This tells us that this particular child is unique and miraculous.

Luke composes an artistic drama, switching back and forth between the births of John the Baptist and Jesus. Undoubtedly, Luke brings Jesus and John together to show their relationship in God's plan of salvation. John's role is to go before Jesus, to herald the advent of the Messiah, to prepare the people for his coming. Jesus, on the other hand, will save the people and rule as king of heaven and earth.

God is involved in their lives from the very beginning. John's conception can be considered miraculous. Elizabeth will conceive a child even though she is an old woman and Zechariah is an old man.

When the angel Gabriel visits Mary and announces that she too is to conceive a child, Mary asks:

> "But how can this come about, since I have no knowledge of man?" (Lk 1:34).

The angel assures Mary that she will conceive in a miraculous way. Her son is one of a kind, God's own son.

> "The Holy Spirit will come upon you, and the power of the most High will cover you with its shadow. And so the child will be holy and will be called Son of God" (Lk 1:35).

Read the following passages from Luke's gospel and note the similarities and differences between the births of John the Baptist and Jesus.

The annunciation of Jesus' birth — 1:5-25
The annunciation of John's birth — 1:26-38

Zechariah's canticle of joy about John's birth — 1:67-79
Mary's canticle of praise about Jesus' birth — 1:46-56

Birth and naming of John — 1:57-66
Birth and naming of Jesus — 2:1-21

John's youth — 1:80
Jesus' youth — 2:39-40

Mary, a quiet, loving girl of perhaps 13 was totally open to God's will. She is the perfect symbol of every person striving for holiness.

> "You see before you the Lord's servant, let it happen to me as you have said" (Lk 1:38).

Matthew tells us that Joseph was dismayed when he discovered that Mary was with child. Mary and Joseph were betrothed. Jewish marriage customs at this time consisted of the betrothal, a formal consent to get married, done before witnesses; and later taking the bride to the groom's family home. The husband did not engage in sexual relations with his betrothed until he took her to his home. Betrothal usually lasted about a year.

Joseph knew that he had not had sexual relations with Mary. Any sexual relations with someone other than one's betrothed was considered the same as adultery. Thus, according to the marriage customs of his day, Joseph had the legal right to separate from Mary. From all appearances, it looked like she had broken her betrothal vows. Although he didn't want to marry her, he was still a just and caring man and he decided to divorce her quietly.

Before he could act, God's messenger appeared to Joseph in a dream and told him that Mary's son was to be the savior of humanity. This humble carpenter adopted Jesus as his son and lived with Mary and Jesus for the rest of his life. Christian tradition teaches that Mary remained a virgin through her whole life.

The virgin birth of Jesus makes a profound statement: *Jesus is unlike any other person ever born. He is both God and human.* The Incarnation, that is, God becoming human in Jesus, is a totally unparalleled event in human history. The good news of our salvation in Jesus Christ begins from the very moment of his conception!

Why? Luke artfully draws out the significance of the birth of Jesus of Nazareth by recounting three religious ceremonies associated with the birth of every firstborn Jewish male.

First, Luke tells us that on the eighth day after Jesus' birth, he had to be circumcised. Circumcision initiated the

Jewish male infant into God's Chosen People. On this occasion, he was given the highly symbolic name *Jesus*, thus foreshadowing his role as savior of all people.

The second and third religious rituals concerned Mary's purification and Jesus' presentation. According to Jewish law, the mother of a child became ritually unclean for seven days after the birth of a son. She was to remain separated from all religious ceremonies for a total of 40 days. At the end of this period, she underwent a rite of purification.

This rite roughly coincided with Jesus' presentation in the Temple for the Jewish rite of redemption. According to Jewish Law, every firstborn male was consecrated to God in thanksgiving for the sparing of firstborn children of the Israelites at the time of the Exodus. Mary and Joseph sacrificed a pair of turtledoves to praise God for his goodness in sending them a son.

An old man named Simeon appears at Jesus' presentation. Luke tells us that the Holy Spirit promised this devout old man that he would not die before meeting the Messiah. Inspired by the Spirit, Simeon went into the Temple area and met the holy family. He took Jesus into his arms and proclaimed the awesome truth of Jesus' birth:

> Now, Master, you are letting your servant go in
>   peace
> as you promised;
> for my eyes have seen the salvation
> which you have made ready in the sight of the
>   nations;
> a light of revelation for the gentiles
> and glory for your people Israel (Lk 2:29-32).

The prophet Simeon shows *why* Jesus' birth is so special: salvation begins with the birth of the Messiah. In a similar way, Luke recounts the story of Anna, an 84-year old prophetess who lived in the Temple region. She also met Jesus and immediately began to praise God. She enthusiastically spread the news that God had begun the deliverance of Jerusalem, the holy city, a symbol for God's Chosen People. Yahweh has kept his promises to the Jewish nation. The Messiah has come!

Simeon and Anna, an old man and an old woman, are the very first to herald the significance of Jesus' birth. And they do this at the very center of Jewish worship and power, the Temple. Their long, faith-filled lives ended in the event they patiently prayed for: the salvation of the world and the redemption of God's Chosen People.

The Childhood of Jesus

We know very little about the "hidden years" of Jesus' life, from the time of his birth to the dramatic beginning of his public life. Both Mark and John begin their gospels with Jesus' baptism. Only Matthew and Luke tell us anything about Jesus' childhood, and what they report is sketchy and, like the infancy narratives, more concerned with symbolism than concrete details.

Matthew tells us the Holy Family fled to Egypt because of Herod's attempt to ferret out and kill the newborn king. Once again God revealed to Joseph in a dream that he was to flee Judea with Jesus and Mary and go to Egypt.

The story of the flight into Egypt is richly symbolic. For example, Jesus' foster father, Joseph, is comparable to the Old Testament patriarch named Joseph who won favor in Egypt. He eventually saved his brothers and the Jewish people by inviting them to Egypt at the time of great famine. Egypt thus became a symbol of salvation for the Chosen People at a critical time in their early history.

Egypt also calls to mind the evil pharaoh at the time of Moses' birth. Pharaoh had ordered the killing of all newborn Hebrew males. Moses' mother hid Moses, who was found and adopted by Pharaoh's daughter. In time he grew up to lead the Hebrew people out of their miserable condition of slavery in Egypt. Herod, like the pharaoh of old, tried to thwart God's plan for Jesus, but without success. Just as Yahweh protected his people by sparing Moses' life, God looked out for all humanity by preserving Jesus' life so he could reveal God's will for us, teach us how to live and then to offer up his life freely when his mission was complete.

Matthew tells us that the Holy Family remained in Egypt until Herod died. They returned to Nazareth sometime during the reign of Herod's son, Archelaus, who ruled Judea from 4 B.C. to A.D. 6.

Luke simply reports that Jesus went to Nazareth with Mary and Joseph and grew to maturity. He succinctly sums up Jesus' youth in these few words:

> Jesus increased in wisdom, in stature, and in favor with God and with people (Lk 2:52).

Everyday Life in Nazareth. What was Jesus' childhood like? We conclude that it was probably similar to other people living in his time and place. His family lived in a cube-like, one-room dwelling, perhaps partly a cave. He would have slept on the floor on a mat, covering himself with a tunic or cloak. His food consisted of wheat or barley bread, fruits, milk, fish, eggs and, on rare occasions, meat. His clothing might have included a linen cloth wrapped around the loins, a short tunic and perhaps a long tunic reaching to the ankles and held together by a girdle (belt).

Jesus spoke the language of his people—Aramaic. This melodious language replaced Hebrew as the everyday spoken language when the Persian Empire reigned supreme. It is still spoken today in some remote villages not too far from Damascus, Syria. Aramaic words like *Golgotha* and *mammon* and expressions like *Abba* and *Talitha, koum* ("Little girl, I tell you to get up"—Mk 5:41) appear in the gospels.

As a boy, Jesus probably rambled up the hills of Nazareth, befriending shepherds and catching glimpses of the beautiful Sea of Galilee gleaming in the distance. His father would certainly have done work for farmers who might well have become family friends. Undoubtedly, too, Jesus got to know some fishermen and their way of life whenever his family traveled to the seashore.

As a child growing up in Galilee Jesus would, of course, have noted with interest the occupying forces of the Roman armies. He would have heard the many hateful expressions uttered by his countrymen against them. Galilee was a notorious hotbed of revolutionary activity against the Romans.

A key element in Jesus' education in Nazareth would have been his religious education. This took place both at home under the guidance of Joseph and Mary and also in

the synagogue. The word *synagogue* means both the people who assemble to worship and the place of assembly. Every town, including Nazareth, had at least one synagogue. People came to the synagogue to pray and to meet and decide community affairs. It also served as the local school and center for religious education.

Most probably Jesus joined other five-year-old boys to begin his formal education. He came to the synagogue where the rabbi (teacher) began to instruct him in the Law. His major education task was to memorize the Law. The Law or Torah is found in the first five books of the Old Testament (the *Pentateuch*).

Jesus also learned carpentry from his foster father, Joseph. A carpenter's ordinary work included cutting wood and making and repairing things like plows and yokes, winnowing forks, threshing sledges, tables, couches and lampstands. On some occasions, Jesus may have helped his father build houses.

The Temple Incident.   Jesus must have been an outstanding student, taking his studies and reflection on the sacred writings most seriously. We can surmise this from Luke's story of a key incident in Jesus' life as an emerging adult. According to the Law, Jewish males had to go to the Jerusalem Temple three times a year to celebrate the pilgrim feasts. Luke tells us that Joseph and Mary went to Jerusalem annually to celebrate the feast of the Passover, which commemorated Israel's deliverance from slavery in Egypt.

At the age of 12, Jesus was now a "son of the Law" and expected to attend the Temple feasts. On the return trip home, Mary and Joseph discovered that he was not traveling in the caravan with them or their relatives. They returned and searched for him for three days.

> They found him in the Temple, sitting among the teachers, listening to them, and asking them questions; and all those who heard him were astounded at his intelligence and his replies. They were overcome when they saw him, and his mother said to him, "My child, why have you done this to us? See how worried

your father and I have been, looking for you." He replied, "Why were you looking for me? Did you not know that I must be in my Father's house?" But they did not understand what he meant (Lk 2: 46-50).

On the symbolic level this story tells us many things. First, Jesus was a practicing Jew. He joyfully celebrated the feasts of his people. Second, he was an excellent student of the holy scriptures and the Law. Luke could have surmised from the brilliant teaching career of Jesus that Jesus must have been an astute student of God's word as a youth. Third, this scene reveals that Jesus belongs to more than just Mary and Joseph. God is his Father; Jesus' family is all people.

Luke closes his story by saying that Jesus returned to Nazareth with Mary and Joseph and lived under their authority. Perhaps during these hidden years of preparation, Jesus' education drove home to him his true identity as God's unique Son whose work he came into the world to accomplish.

Obedience

Luke tells us that Jesus lived his youth as an obedient child to his mother, Mary, and foster father, Joseph. Judge how obedient you are by rating yourself on the following. Answer with one of the following: always (A), usually (U), rarely (R).

_____ When my parents ask me to come home by a certain hour, I honor their request.

_____ I perform household chores promptly and without complaint.

_____ I do homework when told to do so.

_____ I help with younger siblings when asked.

_____ I promptly get off the phone when requested to do so.

· discuss ·

What do you think is a reasonable curfew on non-school nights for a 15-year-old? for a 17-year-old?

Should your parents penalize you (for example, grounding) when you don't honor the curfew they set? Why or why not?

· summary ·

1. Only Matthew and Luke record birth stories about Jesus. Their accounts are primarily *theological* in intent to show that Jesus was special from the moment of his conception.

2. By tracing Jesus' genealogy to Adam, Luke tries to show that Jesus is the universal Messiah. Matthew traced Jesus to Abraham and David to show that Jesus' coming fulfilled all God's promises to the Hebrew people.

3. Jesus was born in Bethlehem, sometime between 4-8 B.C., during the reign of Herod the Great.

4. The name *Jesus* means "Yahweh is salvation." *Christ* is a title that means Messiah.

5. The virginal conception of Jesus shows two things: (1) Jesus is the unique Son of God; (2) He is a human being like us.

6. The infancy narratives underscore the truth that Jesus came to save and liberate all people.

7. The flight of the Holy Family into Egypt symbolizes Yahweh's protection of his Son who came into the world for the specific mission of salvation.

8. The gospels tell us very little about Jesus' childhood and youth, the so-called "hidden years." We know he grew up in Nazareth, learned carpentry from his foster father, and studied the Law in the local synagogue. He lived the typical life of Jewish children of his day.

9. At age 12 Jesus went to Jerusalem to celebrate the Passover with his parents. His family were pious Jews who observed the customary Jewish feasts. Mary did not fully understand Jesus' reference to doing his Father's business.

focus questions

1. Discuss and explain at least two differences in the genealogies of Luke and Matthew.

2. What is the significance behind Jesus being born in Bethlehem? What point does Luke make when the shepherds visit him there? What point does Matthew make in the story of the magi?

3. Why is Jesus' given name especially appropriate? What was his possible surname?

4. Discuss several points of comparison between the birth of John the Baptist and that of his cousin, Jesus. Why does Luke discuss John's birth at the same time as Jesus'?

5. Explain two events associated with Egypt from the history of the Chosen People.

6. How would Jesus have lived as a child and youth? For example: Where did he live? What kind of food did he eat? What was his education like? What language did he speak?

7. Discuss the significance of the Temple episode when Jesus was 12.

8. What is the meaning of each of the following terms?

Annunciation	salvation
evangelist	Torah
Incarnation	virgin birth
Pentateuch	

journal entries

1. Based on what you read in this chapter and any research you might do on the customs of Jewish people in Jesus' day, write a one-page profile of what Jesus would have been like at your age.

2. As a prayer exercise, write Jesus a letter telling him how he has been a gift in your life. What is the greatest thing he has done for you? Also be sure to tell him the greatest thing you have done for him.

3. *Enriching your vocabulary.* Using a good dictionary, look up the meaning of the following terms. Write the definitions in your journal.

ferret out	purport
foreshadow	succinct
pilgrim	surmise
portend	vindictive
precocious	

Prayer Reflection

When Mary heard the news that she was to be God's mother, she prayed the following prayer, the *Magnificat*. This famous Christian prayer teaches the true meaning of humility and doing God's will. Pray it with confidence and faith in God's goodness.

My soul proclaims the greatness of the Lord
and my spirit *rejoices in God my Savior*
because *he has looked upon the humiliation of his servant.*
Yes, from now onwards all generations will call me
    blessed,
for the Almighty has done great things for me.
Holy is his name,
and *his faithful love extends age after age to those who
    fear him.*
He has used the power of his arm,
he has routed the arrogant of heart.
He has pulled down princes from their thrones *and
    raised high the lowly.*
He has filled the starving with good things, sent the rich
    away empty.
*He has come to the help of Israel his servant, mindful of
    his faithful love*
—according to the promise he made to our
ancestors—of his mercy to Abraham and to his
descendants for ever.

—Luke 1:46-55

▪ *reflection* ▪

Jesus has exalted you, too. You are great in his eyes.

▪ *resolution* ▪

Think of one thing you can do for Jesus this week to thank him for the gift of his friendship. Be sure to follow through on your promise.

chapter 3

Jesus Begins His Ministry

The spirit of the Lord is on me,
for he has anointed me
to bring the good news to the afflicted.
He has sent me to proclaim liberty to captives,
sight to the blind,
to let the oppressed go free,
to proclaim a year of favor from the Lord.

—Luke 4:18

In a story about Satan, the Father of Lies lectures some young devils on the best way to deceive people. First, he asked his young recruits what they thought were the best methods of leading people away from God.

The youngest recruit spoke up first. "I think the best way to deceive people is to convince them there is no God."

"That's OK," commented Satan. "This method is called 'The Frontal Attack.' We've been using it for centuries, but without much luck. Very few people have become true atheists."

"Perhaps people could be blinded to the reality of hell," chimed in a second young devil.

Satan shrugged his shoulders. "This method worked well enough in the past couple hundred years or so. Many free-thinkers bought that line. Today, however, many people sense that they will be held accountable for all the war, hatred and callous neglect of others that is floating around. You'll have to suggest something better."

A small, rather ugly little devil was the next to offer his idea. "Instead of trying to convince everyone there is no God, let's try to convince them that God is really a nice guy. He's so laid-back they don't need to make an immediate decision to believe in him."

"Hm," the Prince of Evil mumbled. "Not a bad idea. This is the second most effective temptation. We call it *procrastination.* It works great with young people who think they have all the time in the world. Unfortunately, the old don't buy it."

"For badness sake, then," cried the young devils, "what is the best method of deception?"

"It's really rather easy," replied the Master of Deceit. "The method works with all kinds of people—churchgoers and those who sleep in late or hit the golf courses on Sunday morning. I call it *lukewarmness*. Your job is to convince people not to get too excited about God. Get them to see that too much religion is bad for the soul; but a little bit is better than nothing. If they buy this message, then they'll *think* they're holy. In truth, however, they lack spirit and drive. Yep, lukewarmness works every time."[1]

This story rings true. Christians who are lukewarm in their faith haven't really accepted Jesus or his message. They do not imitate the Lord himself, who burned with a sense of mission and purpose. Jesus was filled with the Spirit. He was passionately committed to revealing God's will. He had high principles and resisted all temptations to mediocrity.

Commitment and Gifts

The Lord wants us to commit ourselves to him with passion so we can continue his work here on earth. To help us serve others, the Holy Spirit has blessed us with many gifts. Jesus challenges his friends to develop and use these gifts for the sake of God's kingdom.

> All of us, though there are so many of us, make up one body in Christ, and as different parts we are all joined to one another. Then since the gifts that we have differ according to the grace that was given to each of us: if it is a gift of prophecy, we should prophesy as much as our faith tells us; if it is a gift of practical service, let us devote ourselves to serving; if it is teaching, to teaching; if it is encouraging, to encouraging. When you give, you should give generously from the heart; if you are put in charge, you must be conscientious; if you do works of mercy, let it be because you enjoy doing them. Let love be without any pretense (Rom 12:5-9).

---

[1] Adapted from William R. White, *Stories for the Journey* (Minneapolis: Augsburg Publishing House, 1988), pp. 25-26.

Judge how well you use the spiritual gifts listed below. (1—weak quality with you; 5—strong quality with you.)

Speaking God's Word

The Lord has given me a gift of sharing his word with others. I can speak the truth honestly and joyfully. Others seem to find comfort in my words.

1   2   3   4   5

Service

I am sensitive to others' needs and respond in some concrete way to help them out.

1   2   3   4   5

Teaching

The Lord has given me an ability to help others learn. I can explain things well.

1   2   3   4   5

Encouraging

I have a real gift of seeing the good in others and in helping them see it, too.

1   2   3   4   5

Generosity

God has blessed me with the ability to let go and share myself—time, things, friendship—with others.

1   2   3   4   5

Leadership

I have leadership ability—a way of organizing people to get things done. I am also dependable when put in charge of something.

1   2   3   4   5

Compassion

The Lord has given me the ability to sense when someone is hurting, and he has given me the courage to respond in a loving way.

1   2   3   4   5

■ *journal* ■

Reflect on the gifts the Lord has given you. List some ways you can concretely use these gifts to help those you meet each day.

Jesus' Baptism

> It was at this time that Jesus came from Nazareth in Galilee and was baptized in the Jordan by John. And at once, as he was coming up out of the water, he saw the heavens torn apart and the Spirit, like a dove, descending on him. And a voice came from heaven, "You are my Son, the Beloved; my favor rests on you" (Mk 1:9-11).

All four gospels agree on an important point: Jesus began his public ministry by accepting baptism at the hand of John the Baptist. The beginning of Jesus' ministry, therefore, was intimately tied into that of his kinsman, John the Baptist.

Who Was John the Baptist?   Luke tells us that John the Baptist came on the scene during the 15th year of the Roman emperor Tiberius' reign. The historical-minded Luke also records that Herod Antipas was ruling in Galilee, Jesus' home region. He also reports that Herod's brother, Philip, controlled the regions of Ituraea and Trachonitis. In addition, Luke mentions three men who were to figure prominently in the death of Jesus: the Roman procurator Pontius Pilate had authority in Judea and the high-priest-hood of the Temple was under the control of Annas and Caiaphas. These details fix both John the Baptist and the beginning of Jesus' public ministry within the political scene of the day.

The gospels tell us that John was the precursor of the Messiah. He came to prepare people spiritually for the marvelous work God was about to begin in Jesus. John was a forceful preacher, one who challenged his hearers to reform their lives:

> "Brood of vipers, who warned you to flee from the coming retribution? Produce fruit in keeping with repentance" (Lk 3:7-8).

In response to their question "What must we do?" John challenged his hearers to share their clothing and food with the poor. He told tax collectors to exact no more than what was owed. He instructed soldiers to be gentle with people and to be content with their salary. Furthermore, John had the courage to condemn publicly the behavior of King Herod Antipas who had married Herodias, his brother's wife. This so incensed Herod that he eventually arrested John and had him beheaded.

John was an attractive personality. Many of the Jewish people thought he was himself the Messiah, the promised one. John replied:

> "I baptize you with water, but someone is coming, who is more powerful than me, and I am not fit to undo the strap of his sandals; he will baptize you with the Holy Spirit and fire" (Lk 3:16).

The gospel writers tell us that John wore a garment of camel's hair and a leather belt. He ate grasshoppers and wild honey. The informed reader would realize that Luke is describing Elijah here, a great Old Testament prophet. The Old Testament prophesied that Elijah would return to precede the Messiah and announce his coming.

Why Did John Baptize? Baptisms for recent converts and daily ritual washings by some Jewish groups for religious purification were fairly common in Jesus' day. John only baptized once. In fact, John's baptism was so unique that he was called the Baptist to distinguish his ministry from that of others.

John baptized in the Jordan River, a symbol for Jewish freedom. After the Exodus from Egypt and 40 years of penance and suffering wandering in the desert, the Chosen People entered the Promised Land. Crossing the Jordan was a final step in Yahweh's plan to give his people their own land.

Baptism by John in the Jordan was a dramatic sign of his followers' willingness to become like their ancient ancestors. It symbolized their turn from self-centered sinfulness to an openness to God's word about to be spoken in their day. John's baptism was a sign of their need to be cleansed from sin to prepare for the Lord's coming.

Why Did Jesus Get Baptized?   If John's baptism was a concrete sign of turning from sin to be open to the Messiah when he came, then why would Jesus come to the Jordan River, some 70 miles or so from his home?

Undoubtedly, Jesus came to the Jordan because his time of preparation was over. After prayer and reflection, the Holy Spirit led Jesus to the Jordan where John baptized him. Thus, the sinless savior identified with all people in their spiritual need. He took on the identity of his people as he was immersed in the waters of the Jordan.

When Jesus emerged from the water, the gospels report three phenomena: the *opening of the sky*, the *descent of the Spirit* and a *voice* identifying Jesus. We can make three points about the significance of these images at Jesus' baptism:

1) The opening of the sky signifies that God has come to his people in Jesus. His mission is about to begin.

2) The dove is a symbol of joy, innocence, freedom, power and peace all combined into one rich image. It suggests the dawn of a new age, a new era under the influence and direction of God's spirit.

3) The voice proclaiming "This is my Son, the Beloved" recalls the words of two Old Testament prophecies. Psalm 2:7 promises the coming of the anointed king, the Messiah:

> I will proclaim the decree of Yahweh:
> He said to me, "You are my son,
> today have I fathered you."

Furthermore, the prophet Isaiah tells us:

> Here is my servant whom I uphold,
> my chosen one in whom my soul delights.
> I have sent my spirit upon him (Is 42:1).

Jesus' baptism reveals who he is and what his mission is to be. It shows Jesus is about his Father's work of salvation, a work accomplished by the power of the Holy Spirit. Jesus' baptism foreshadows Christian baptism, which is done in the name of the Father, the Son and the Holy Spirit, so the Lord's work can continue through his followers.

Jesus' Baptism — Varying Accounts

While all the gospel writers report the sky opening, the dove and the voice at Jesus' baptism, they don't agree on the details of these phenomena. Depending on which gospel you read, the experience after Jesus' baptism is either a private event that Jesus later revealed to his apostles or a public event that was seen by all present at the time. Because of the inconsistencies, we can't tell for sure who really witnessed these events. Please read the following accounts of Jesus' baptism. Record the following information in the chart provided.

Who sees the sky opened?
Who sees the dove descending?
Who hears the voice of the Father?

Matthew 3:13-17	Mark 1:9-11	Luke 3:21-22	John 1:29-34

The Temptations of Jesus

For the high priest we have is not incapable of feeling our weaknesses with us, but has been put to the test in exactly the same way as ourselves, apart from sin. Let us, then, have no fear in approaching the throne of grace to receive mercy and to find grace when we are in need of help.

—Hebrews 4:15-16

The author of the letter to the Hebrews tells us that Jesus' own temptations help him identify with humanity. He can sympathize with us because he was tempted like us in every way, except that he never sinned. Temptation to sin is not the same as sin itself. In the Old Testament, the Hebrew word for temptation meant "to try" or "to test." Temptation forces people to respond, showing what they will or can do in a given situation.

Temptation may show our strength of character, but we should not look for temptation to prove ourselves. In his letter to the Galatians, St. Paul warns us to be on guard and avoid all temptations. Jesus himself taught his apostles to pray that they may not fall into temptation. Jesus knew us so well when he said, "The spirit is willing enough, but human nature is weak" (Mk 14:38).

The New Testament frequently images Satan or the devil as the one who tempts us. In the gospels, we see a specific example of Jesus being tempted in the desert and withstanding those temptations.

Obviously, there was no eyewitness to Jesus' temptations. Mark simply records that Satan tempted him. Luke and Matthew, however, tell us the nature of Jesus' three tests. Jesus may have told his disciples of these temptations. Or the gospel writers may have summarized in this story the kinds of temptations Jesus experienced throughout his whole life. Please read either Matthew 4:1-11 or Luke 4:1-13. Then study the chart given below.

Filled with the Holy Spirit, Jesus left the Jordan and was led by the Spirit into the desert, for forty days being put to the test by the devil.

—Luke 4:1-2

Temptation	Jesus' Response	Symbolic Meaning
Turn stone into bread.	*"Human beings live not on bread alone."* —Luke 4:4	Jesus refuses to work a miracle to satisfy his own human needs. He trusts his Father to provide for him. He will use his personal power as God's Son for others.

| If Jesus does homage to Satan, he will gain all the world's power. | *"You must do homage to the Lord your God, him alone you must serve."* —Luke 4:8 | Jesus refuses to seek worldly power. He resists the crowd's appeal to him to be a military or political leader. Instead, he chooses to be a king who serves through suffering and service. |
| If Jesus jumps off the parapet of the Temple the angels will rescue him and he will prove that he is God's Son. | *"Do not put the Lord your God to the test."* —Luke 4:12 | Jesus refuses to test God. He knows his Father. Jesus will not perform a spectacular deed just so people will believe in him. He wants to touch people's hearts and have them believe in him out of true faith. |

Jesus' temptations parallel those of the ancient Israelites in the desert. They gave in to sensuality, fulfilling their own appetites. They bowed down and worshipped false gods in the form of statues. They tried to test God to do their will. Jesus, the new Israel, remained faithful to his Father. Also, Jesus is the new Adam. He refuses to believe in the false promises of the evil one. Instead of being destroyed by Satan, Jesus conquers him.

Jesus' retreat in the desert helped him to clarify who he was as God's Son and what his mission was to be. His test set the course for his future life. As God-made-human, Jesus rejected the easy way out. He would fight evil through a life of gentle, compassionate service of others. He would embrace the suffering involved in his mission of truth and service. He would invite people to believe in him because he is God's Son. Satan promises the easy way out; Jesus shows that love is tough and demanding but the only way to go.

Handling Temptation

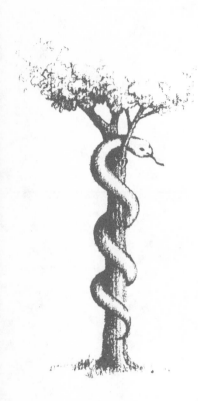

All of us are tempted on a daily basis to be less than we are called to be. We are God's children, brothers and sisters to each other. When we sin, we forget who we are. We act in ways contrary to our true identity.

Here is a list of some common temptations that may beset you over the course of a day. This list corresponds to the traditional seven deadly vices, that is, habits that destroy our relationship with God and others. Judge how well you resist these vices by marking the space provided according to the following scale.

1 — this is not a problem with me

2 — this is a problem, but I usually am able to handle it

3 — this is a problem, and I need some work to resist this particular temptation

_____ 1. PRIDE: I think that I am better than my classmates.

_____ 2. COVETOUSNESS: Acquiring material things grabs a lot of my attention. I am stingy with my possessions.

_____ 3. LUST: I have a tendency to give in to my sexual desires, sometimes even seeking things like pornography to excite them. I rarely try to control my thoughts. I tend to be self-indulgent.

_____ 4. ANGER: I have a short fuse. I let things bother me and take it out on others.

_____ 5. GLUTTONY: I have a tendency to indulge every whim. I do everything to excess. I can't say no to my appetites.

_____ 6. ENVY: The good fortune of others brings out the worst in me. I tear them down or speak ill of them. I am sarcastic and critical.

_____ 7. SLOTH: Laziness is my middle name. I slack off on homework and jobs around the house. I take the easy way out.

Here is a list of seven Christian virtues that offset each of the vices above. Match the number of the vice with the corresponding virtue. Copy the seven Christian virtues into your journal and write a definition for each one.

_____ Chastity   _____ Temperance

_____ Agape-love   _____ Liberality

_____ Humility   _____ Gentleness

_____ Diligence

Jesus Begins His Ministry

After his bout with Satan, Jesus was filled with the power of the Holy Spirit. Matthew tells us that Jesus left the desert after Herod Antipas arrested John the Baptist. John's arrest probably made it clear to Jesus that it was time for him to begin his own ministry.

Jesus returned to his home territory of Galilee, where he immediately began to preach. Mark gives us an excellent summary of Jesus' preaching:

> "The time is fulfilled, and the kingdom of God is close at hand. Repent, and believe the gospel" (Mk 1:15).

Jesus Calls His First Apostles.   Both Matthew and Mark tell us that Jesus was walking by the Lake of Galilee when he saw Simon and Andrew, two brothers who were fishermen. He looked at them and challenged them:

> "Come after me and I will make you fishers of people" (Mt 4:19).

They dropped what they were doing and followed Jesus. Shortly after, Jesus saw another set of brothers—John and James, Zebedee's sons. Jesus called them to follow him; they, too, obeyed, leaving both their father and their nets behind.

In these early days of Jesus' preaching ministry, the gospels tell us that Jesus went around Galilee to teach in the synagogues. He performed many miracles, healing those who were suffering from diseases. He cured the possessed, epileptics and the crippled. Before long, Jesus' reputation spread all over Palestine and into the neighboring regions of Syria, Transjordan and the Decapolis.

During this period, Jesus made Capernaum his headquarters, probably staying in Peter's house. After a time, he decided to return to Nazareth, his home town, to preach God's message. His reputation had preceded him there.

Jesus in Nazareth.   Luke's version of Jesus' early ministry states that Jesus went home almost right away. Once there he went to the synagogue on the Sabbath, as he usually did. It was his turn to do the reading. When handed the scroll, Jesus searched until he found this selection from the prophet Isaiah:

> *The spirit of the Lord is on me,*
> *for he has anointed me*
> *to bring the good news to the afflicted.*
> *He has sent me to proclaim liberty to captives,*
> *sight to the blind,*
> *to let the oppressed go free,*
> *to proclaim a year of favor from the Lord*   (Lk 4:18).

Jesus then rolled up the scroll and gave it back to the attendant and sat down. His reading made a dramatic impact. Everyone was looking at him. They were waiting for him to give a homily on the reading. Jesus did so in one short sentence,

> "This text is being fulfilled today even while you are listening" (Lk 4:21).

At first, Jesus' explanation amazed his audience. His townsfolk marveled at what he said. No one could miss the significance of his message. He proclaimed, in effect, that Isaiah's prophecy about the Messiah was actually coming true—right *now*, in their very midst!

But then it dawned on someone. "This is Joseph's son, surely?" (Lk 4:23). Could Jesus be implying that he is himself the Messiah? People were in an uproar.

Jesus defended himself by saying that no prophet is honored in his own country. He also told two stories about how the Old Testament prophets Elijah and Elisha left Israel to minister to foreigners.

No one missed what Jesus meant. He was suggesting that God's people would reject the Messiah and that God would take his message to the Gentiles. This enraged his townsfolk. They rose in arms against Jesus, drove him from the synagogue, and took him to the brow of a hill with the intent to throw him off. Miraculously, though, Jesus escaped the crowd and walked away because his time to die had not yet arrived.

This incident at Nazareth teaches an important lesson about Jesus. The people really want to accept the Messiah; they want to believe that he has come. However, they were expecting a flashy, forceful military leader. They simply could not see how an ordinary carpenter, who lived in their own village, could possibly be Yahweh's promised one. Jesus was too much like them. He was so ordinary.

Jesus, though, shows how God works through, and is present in, the things of ordinary life. He takes us by surprise. His ways are not our ways. Jesus was asking his townsfolk, "Are you willing to be open-minded enough to be surprised by God?" Jesus asks us the same question today.

▪ *journal* ▪

Do one of the following.

1. Write about a time in your life when God took you by surprise. Explain how he came to you in an ordinary, unexpected way.

2. Write about a time when you took a public stand on an important issue, even though it brought you a lot of criticism. What did you *feel* like? Relate your feelings to what Jesus must have felt when people who grew up with him tried to get rid of him.

You may wish to share this reflection with your classmates.

The Apostles.   Luke tells us that after Jesus left Nazareth, he went to Capernaum. There he taught in the synagogue, healed a possessed man, cured Peter's mother-in-law and many other people as well.

After preaching around Galilee and even into Judea and performing many miracles, Jesus inevitably gathered many disciples. The word *disciple* means apprentice, student, follower. From among these, Jesus selected his twelve apostles to help him in his work. The term *apostle* comes from the Greek word that means "to send." The number of apostles was the same as the number of tribes of Israel, a symbolic number that suggests Jesus came to preach his message to Israel first.

Jesus selected the Twelve after a night of prayer on the mountain. Most of the apostles were humble, lower-class folks, but they were skilled at various crafts or trades. To them, Jesus was like a rabbi or teacher of that time. He expected them to learn carefully from his words and actions so they could pass his message on to others.

Jesus' relationship to his apostles differed in two ways from the rabbi-student relationship. First, *Jesus* chose the apostles; rabbinical students, on the other hand, chose which teacher they wanted to study under. Second, Jesus, unlike any other rabbi, taught on his own authority, directly interpreting the will of his Father. Rabbis of his day were rigorously trained by other rabbis to interpret the Law. They based their opinions on the teachings of others. Jesus was unique. He spoke for God rather than about God, and relied on the authority of no other human being.

The twelve apostles were:

Peter, Simon, the fisherman. Jesus named him Peter, which means "rock." He was the leader of the apostles. Peter was the first to declare Jesus' true identity.

Andrew, also a fisherman, was Peter's brother. John's gospel tells us that Andrew was Jesus' first disciple and that he encouraged his brother to come to Jesus.

James, Zebedee's Son. He and his brother were both fishermen. James became the leader of the Christian community in Jerusalem after the resurrection. Herod Agrippa beheaded him in A.D. 44.

John, Zebedee's Son.   Many scholars believe John was the so-called "beloved disciple" of John's gospel. He was the source of the Fourth Gospel and the Epistles named after him.

Philip,   from Bethsaida, asks Jesus at the Last Supper to show the apostles the Father, to which Jesus replies: "Anyone who has seen me has seen the Father" (Jn 14:9).

Bartholomew.   This apostle is probably the same as the Nathaniel in John's gospel. *Bartholomew* means "son of Thalmai" and may have been Nathaniel's surname.

Matthew.   Levi and Matthew are probably the same person. He was a tax-collector by profession. Tradition holds that in the 40s he wrote a gospel in Aramaic, on which the New Testament's gospel according to Matthew may have been based.

Thomas.   John's gospel calls Thomas "The Twin." He would not believe that Jesus had risen from the dead until he saw him. Tradition also holds that he preached in India, where he was martyred.

James, Son of Alphaeus.   Mark's gospel calls him James the younger, perhaps to distinguish him from James, Zebedee's son.

Simon the Zealot.   The Zealots were a group of revolutionaries who worked to overthrow Roman rule in Palestine through violent means. By following Jesus, Simon had to give up these notions since Jesus was the "Prince of Peace."

Judas, Son of James.   This Judas is also known as **Jude**. Matthew and Mark call him **Thaddeus**, probably a surname, so as not to confuse him with Judas Iscariot, the traitor.

Judas Iscariot.   Each of the gospels calls Judas a traitor. He betrayed Jesus for 30 pieces of silver, and when he realized the magnitude of what he did, he hung himself.

Jesus, the Miracle-Worker

> That evening, after sunset, they brought to him all
> who were sick and those who were possessed by dev-
> ils. The whole town came crowding round the door,
> and he cured many who were sick with diseases of
> one kind or another; he also drove out many devils
> (Mk 1:32-34).

The gospels make it clear that when Jesus began his public life, he performed wonder-works, miracles. They were
a mainstay of his ministry. In fact, they are critically important elements in telling Jesus' story. In Mark's gospel, for
example, half the treatment of Jesus' public life deals with
miracles.

We can distinguish four major categories of miracles in
Jesus' ministry.

1. *Physical healings.* Jesus was a healer who enabled the
   blind to see, the deaf to hear, the lame to walk. He cured
   leprosy and healed a woman with a long-term
   hemorrhage.

2. *Nature miracles.* Jesus demonstrated mastery over the
   elements. For example, he calmed a storm and walked
   on water. He cursed a fig tree, causing it to wither. He
   also performed miracles over things. He fed five thou-
   sand people when he multiplied five loaves and two
   fish. He changed water into wine.

3. *Exorcisms.* An exorcism is the expulsion of evil spirits
   that possess a person, place or object. In Jesus' day,
   these spirits tormented people and sometimes drove
   them crazy. Jesus drove a legion of spirits out of a crazy
   man, sending them into a herd of swine that ran off a
   cliff. On several other occasions he cast demons out of
   people who were possessed.

4. *Raising from the dead.* The gospels report several examples of Jesus bringing a dead person back to life, for
   example, the widow's son at Nain and the daughter of
   Jairus. Finally, he brought back to life his friend Lazarus,
   whose corpse lay rotting in the grave.

Are Miracles Believable?   Some people today, influenced by a sophisticated world-view and modern science, have great difficulty accepting that Jesus performed any miracles at all. They understand the concept of *miracle* to be "a suspension of the laws of nature." To their way of thinking, God does not get involved in the natural universe. They believe science will one day be able to explain the unexplainable, the apparently miraculous.

Modern-day skeptics either don't believe in Jesus' miracles or they try to explain them away. For example, they might say that Jesus was like a psychiatrist. He knew what emotional disorders were afflicting people who came to him; he merely said the right words to make them mentally well. Or they give a symbolic interpretation to a nature miracle like the multiplication of the loaves and fishes. For example, they say that the real "miracle" was that the little boy shared his food. His example caught on and inspired the rest of the crowd to share their food among themselves. Or Jesus brought people back to life who were only in a deep coma. According to this explanation, Jesus knew a form of artificial respiration that revived an apparently dead person.

Even people in Jesus' day who witnessed what he did right before their eyes refused to believe. John's gospel tells us about a man Jesus cured of his blindness. Some of Jesus' opponents simply claimed that the man was never blind to begin with.

The Nature of Jesus' Miracles.   There were other healers in Jesus' day in both the Jewish and Roman world. Jesus' contemporaries believed that God-inspired people had the ability to perform healings. The New Testament itself mentions people who had the power to heal.

Jesus' miracles stand out, though, among those of other wonder–workers of his day. First, there is no record that anyone else cured such a variety of problems. Second, Jesus did not engage in any bizarre rituals to bring about the cures as did so many of his contemporaries. He healed on his own authority, using his own power, often stressing the need for the afflicted to have faith. Finally, Jesus did not perform miracles for pay. He did them out of the goodness of his heart.

To understand the meaning of Jesus' miracles, we have to look at them from the biblical perspective. The Bible has a religious understanding of miracle. It assumes that God cares for us and continues to work in human history through events we call miraculous, as well as in more ordinary ways.

The New Testament uses two different but related words to express the concept of miracle. The gospels of Matthew, Mark and Luke use the word *dynamis*; John uses the word *semeion*. *Dynamis* (compare the English words *dynamic* and *dynamite*) means "power." *Semeion* means "sign." Let's look at what these words convey about Jesus and his message.

The blind see again . . .
the lame walk . . .
the deaf hear . . .
the dead are raised to life . . .
the good news is proclaimed to
  the poor.
—Luke 7:22-23

Jesus' miracles reveal God's power:

- *In and through Jesus, God's power has broken into human history.* As the creator of everything, God is the ruler of nature. When Jesus calms the storm, for example, he demonstrates that he is closely identified with Yahweh who is the master of the universe. The miracles help show who Jesus is and where he comes from.

- *Jesus has mastery over Satan and the forces of darkness.* When Jesus drives out demons, for example, he proclaims that God has power over sickness and the evil it brings. When he raises someone from the dead, Jesus shows that he has power over the worst evil of all—death. Jesus crushes Satan's power.

- *Jesus has power to forgive sins.* Sin separates people from God and one another. It makes us hate ourselves, others and God. It leads to death. When Jesus forgives sin, he speaks for God. He helps free people from the alienation that causes spiritual suffering and death. His opponents criticize him for forgiving sin because only God can forgive sin. Jesus performs miracles to show that he has the power to forgive sin. He is God.

- *Miracles reveal Jesus' identity.* Anyone who has God's power over nature, over sickness and death, over Satan and the forces of evil, over sin itself, must *be* God. The miracles show that Jesus is God's son!

Jesus' miracles are signs of the coming of God's reign:

- *Jesus forcefully proves God's love and compassion through the miracles.* A key sign of God's presence in the world is concern for the lowly, the sick, the outcasts. For example, when Jesus associates with the lepers—who were despised and avoided because of their disease—he proclaims that God cares. When he cures them of this disease, he shows that God takes pity on his people.

- *God's kingdom is here; Satan's kingdom is ending.* Sin, sickness and death entered the world when Adam sinned. Jesus is the new Adam who inaugurates God's reign over human hearts. The miracles are the sign of the advent of God's reign. When John the Baptist sent his friends to ask Jesus if he was indeed the promised Messiah, Jesus sent back the following answer:

> "Go back and tell John what you have seen and heard: the blind see again, the lame walk, those suffering from virulent skin-diseases are cleansed, and the deaf hear, the dead are raised to life, the good news is proclaimed to the poor; and blessed is anyone who does not find me a cause of falling" (Lk 7:22-23).

The miracles prompt people to put their faith in Jesus. Jesus taught that he was the way, the truth and the life. He performed miracles as a response to faith in him. For example, he raised Lazarus because his sister Martha proclaimed her faith in him.

> "I am the resurrection.
> Anyone who believes in me, even though that
>   person dies, will live,
> and whoever lives and believes in me
> will never die.
> Do you believe this?"
>
> "Yes, Lord," she said (Jn 11:25-27).

Jesus raised Lazarus in one of his most significant miracles, a powerful sign that Jesus has power to conquer death; it symbolizes that through Jesus our own resurrection takes place. Our ultimate salvation—conquering our own death—comes through Jesus. He is the resurrection and the life. Without him we are dead.

John's gospel reports that many Jews believed in Jesus after witnessing this miracle. But some went to the Pharisees, who along with the chief priests, plotted Jesus' death. Miracles force people to ask some basic questions: "Is Jesus the sign we have been looking for? Is he the promised one? Is he the Messiah? If he is, then we will have to change our lives and follow him." Jesus' miracles help us to face and answer the question: "Who do *you* say that I am?"

Miracles of Jesus

Here is a list of some key miracles of Jesus. Do the following exercise in your notebook. Discuss the results with your classmates.

1. Please read one version of each miracle. Note what has taken place on the surface level; for example, Jesus cures a man's blindness.

2. Then interpret the deeper meaning of the miracle. How does it show God's *power*? How is it a *sign* of God's reign? For example, in the case of the blind man, you might say that God's power makes people see the true light. Or you might conclude that faith in Jesus enabled him to see God working through his Son who enables us to walk in the light.

3. With your classmates, compare and contrast the various versions of the miracles you have studied.

	Matthew	Mark	Luke	John
Healing Miracles				
The blind man (men) of Jericho	20:29-34	10:46-52	18:35-43	
The leper in Capernaum	8:2-4	1:40-45	5:12-14	

Nature Miracles

Multiplication of loaves and fishes	14:13-21	6:30-44	9:10-17	6:1–15
Calming of the storm	8:23-27	4:35-41	8:22-25	

Exorcisms

The demoniac		1:23-28	4:33-37	
Possessed mute	9:32-34		11:14-15	

Raisings from the dead

Widow's son			7:11-16	
Jairus' daughter	9:18-26	5:21-43	8:40-56	

▪ *Summary* ▪

1. John the Baptist, Jesus' kinsman, was the precursor of the Messiah. He preached a message of repentance in preparation for the coming of the Messiah.

2. Jesus accepted baptism at John's hands to identify with the spiritual condition of all people.

3. Jesus' baptism reveals who he is as God's Son. It signals the beginning of his Messianic mission as a suffering servant.

4. After Jesus was baptized he went into the desert to pray, to fast and to prepare for his mission.

5. The temptations of Jesus reveal that Jesus resisted the easy way out. His public mission was to be the hard road of love. He refuses to work miracles to serve his own ends. He does not accept political power. He does not perform miracles to force faith. In all cases, Jesus lovingly shows that he trusts his Father.

6. Jesus began his ministry by proclaiming the coming of God's reign. He called for repentance and for faith in the gospel.

7. Jesus was rejected in his own home town of Nazareth. Undoubtedly his townsfolk had difficulty seeing God's presence in one of their own. Even today God works

Jesus went into Galilee. There he proclaimed the gospel from God saying, "The time is fulfilled and the kingdom of God is close at hand. Repent, and believe the gospel."

—Mark 1:14-15

through ordinary events. It takes faith to recognize his presence.

8. Jesus chose and formed 12 apostles to carry on his work after his death and resurrection. Unlike other teachers of his day, Jesus chose his own students (disciples) and taught on his own authority.

9. Miracles played an important part in Jesus' ministry. They prove God's *power* over sin, sickness and death. They show who Jesus is as God's Son and that he has power over Satan. They reveal God's compassion for us and are a principal *sign* of his reign. Jesus' miracles invite us to have faith in him as our Lord and Messiah.

▪ *focus questions* ▪

1. Who was John the Baptist? How did he figure in Jesus' ministry? Why did he baptize?
2. Identify the following people:

    Annas   Caiaphas   Herodias
3. Why did Jesus get baptized?
4. What were the three temptations of Jesus? What did each mean?
5. What are the seven deadly vices? Give an example of each one.
6. Why didn't Jesus' own people want to accept him?
7. Who were the 12 apostles? Say something about each one.
8. What are the four categories of miracles Jesus performed? Give an example of each kind.
9. How do some people today view the idea of miracles? How does the Bible understand the concept of miracle? Explain the meaning of miracle as *power* and *sign*.
10. Why did Jesus perform miracles? What did they reveal about him and his mission?
11. How did Jesus differ from other wonder-workers of his day?
12. What is the meaning of each of the following terms?

    apostle   disciple   miracle

▪ *journal entries* ▪

1. Ask at least two adults if they believe in miracles. Write up the results of your interview in your journal.

2. Jesus prayed before making decisions. Write about a time when prayer helped you decide something or helped you figure something out.

3. *Enriching your vocabulary.*   Using a good dictionary, look up the meaning of the following terms. Write the definitions in your journal.

alienation	indulgent
callous	pornography
conscientious	retribution
diligence	temptation
exorcism	virulent

Prayer Reflection

He said to them, "When you pray, this is what to say . . . "
—Luke 11:2

Jesus showed that prayer was important in his life. He also taught us how to pray. Recite with feeling the prayer he gave to us.

"In your prayers do not babble as the gentiles do, for they think that by using many words they will make themselves heard. Do not be like them; your Father knows what you need before you ask him. So you should pray like this:

Our Father in heaven,
may your name be held holy,
your kingdom come,
your will be done,
on earth as in heaven.
Give us today our daily bread.
And forgive us our debts,
as we have forgiven those who are in debt to us.
And do not put us to the test,
but save us from the Evil One.

"Yes, if you forgive others their failings, your heavenly Father will forgive you yours; but if you do not forgive others, your Father will not forgive your failings either."

—Matthew 6:7-15

. *reflection* .

We don't have to use a lot of words to pray. We only need to approach God simply, like a little child approaches his or her parents to ask for something.

. *resolution* .

Jesus tells us to pray with forgiveness in our hearts. Who has hurt you and needs your forgiveness? Approach this person soon and extend the healing touch of forgiveness. Whom have you hurt? Can you ask this person to forgive you?

Chapter 4

Jesus and His People

"Do not imagine that I have come to abolish the Law or the Prophets. I have come not to abolish but to complete them. In truth I tell you, till heaven and earth disappear, not one dot, not one little stroke, is to disappear from the Law until all its purpose is achieved."

—Matthew 5:17-18

In This Chapter

We will look at:

- the story of Jesus' people
- religious groups in Jesus' day

Imagine the following scene. Some young boys are playing. One boy asks his companions to join him in a footrace. One of the boys says he doesn't want to compete. He begins to walk slowly away from the rest, but is stopped by the boy who suggested the race. What do you think will happen next?

Or picture this scene. A handsome young man walks by the house of a beautiful young lady almost every day. He is healthy, intelligent and strong. He does not have a wife, but would very much like to marry and raise a family. The young woman is sweet, charming and intelligent. She, too, is unmarried and would love to have someone ask for her hand in marriage. They know each other well, but even though they like each other, neither has ever mentioned marriage. Why?

What happens to the little boy who does not want to race? Absolutely nothing. He is a Navaho Indian. In his culture, competition is frowned on. None of his playmates would think less of him for not joining in their race.

How about the young couple? They won't marry because they are members of different castes in the Hindu religion. A person from the upper caste is forbidden to marry someone from an inferior caste. As far as marriage is concerned, this man and woman are worlds apart.

To understand someone fully, we must know the customs of their people. So it is with Jesus, who lived in a different time and place than us. In studying Jesus, we have

73

to remember that Jesus was a Jew who grew up with and was formed in the faith of his people. He kept the Law, prayed in the synagogue, worshipped on the holy days in the Temple and practiced many other Jewish customs of his day. We can't begin to understand who Jesus is without appreciating the story of Yahweh's Chosen People, our ancestors in faith.

Who You Are

Like Jesus, you are a product of your experiences and those who have loved and educated you. Think about influences that have helped make you the person you are.

What is your nationality?

What do you most like about this ethnic group?

What was the most significant event in your life so far? Explain how it might have changed you?

▪ *discuss* ▪

Share your answers with your classmates. See how much you have in common with them.

How might Jesus have answered each of these questions.

The Story of Jesus' People

Jesus' teaching ministry began with these words of good news:

> "The time is fulfilled, and the kingdom of God is close
> at hand. Repent, and believe the gospel" (Mk 1:15).

His people knew what he was talking about because they lived in the hope of God's coming reign. They longed for God's rule, and they expected a Messiah or a ruler to come and establish that rule for God.

To understand the importance of Jesus' proclamation, we must enter into the story of Jesus' people. Their story is our story, too. The central theme of this story is the covenant. Yahweh selected this group of people to favor with

▪ *journal* ▪

In your journal, make three lists. In the first, list five things you are proud of about yourself. In the second, list five things you are proud of about your family. In the final list, mention five things you most admire about Jesus. Then write a paragraph to explain your choices for any two of the 15 things you listed.

his protection and love. In return, they were to obey God's law and live just and faithful lives. This contract or covenant began at the time of Abraham and was fulfilled in Jesus.

1. *Abraham's call (c. 1900 B.C.):*   Many centuries ago, God said to a wandering herdsman:

> "Leave your country, your kindred and your father's house for a country which I shall show you; and I shall make you a great nation, I shall bless you and make your name famous; you are to be a blessing!
>
> > I shall bless those who bless you,
> > and shall curse those who curse you,
> > and all clans on earth
> > will bless themselves by you."

So Abram went as Yahweh told him (Gn 12:1-4).

God called Abraham from the desert to create a people, his Chosen People. God initiated the covenant with Abraham; he extended the call. However, Abraham had to say yes and obey God's command for Israel to become God's people. Abraham had to believe.

Jesus calls on his followers to believe, too. For Jesus, Abraham is the key symbol of faith:

> "If you are Abraham's children,
> do as Abraham did" (Jn 8:39).

Abraham showed courageous faith in following the word of God. Because he left the secure life he had known, God blessed him with a family and a land. His grandson Jacob (later named Israel) raised a family north of Palestine. One of Jacob's sons, Joseph, was sold into Egypt as a slave. Joseph's intelligence got him a position of influence that enabled him to settle his family in Egypt when there was famine in their native land. Jacob's descendants, the Israelites, grew in number. The Egyptians feared them and forced them to do hard labor.

2. *Exodus experience (c. 1250 B.C.):*   The Exodus was the most significant event in Jewish history. God delivered his people from slavery in Egypt under the able leadership of

Read Gen 12, 15, 17.

Where did Abraham go at the time of the famine?

What covenant did God make with Abraham? What was the sign of this covenant?

the prophet Moses. This event revealed to the Israelites that Yahweh was a God of unlimited love. All later generations of Jews celebrate the Exodus in the feast of Passover. Jesus himself celebrated Passover with his disciples on the eve of his crucifixion. He saw his own death as the new exodus, which would deliver all people from sin and death and win for them eternal life.

God's love manifested in the Exodus experience freed the Jews from slavery and gave them new life. His care for them in the Sinai desert showed them that he would sustain them and keep them in his loving care. In return for these blessings, Yahweh wanted his Chosen People to believe in him and to commit their lives to him. So God gave them the Law on Mount Sinai, summarized in the Ten Commandments. By living this Law, God's people were to witness to the one true God. Through faithful worship and just lives they were to show what God intended for all people.

Read Ex 19–20.

What covenant did God make on Mount Sinai?

How did God show himself to the Israelites when he gave the terms of this covenant?

Keeping the Covenant

Yahweh wanted the Chosen People to live the Ten Commandments as a sign that they were his special people. Jesus taught that his followers must also keep these commandments. (Reread Exodus 20:1-17.) Here they are in brief form. Examine how well you uphold your part of the covenant, the invitation to be a member of God's people.

1 — I do this well
2 — I usually do this
3 — I sometimes do this
4 — I need improvement

Commandment

_____ 1. God is the #1 priority in my life.

_____ 2. I use God's name with reverence.

_____ 3. I worship God on his special day and otherwise keep this day holy.

_____ 4. I honor and obey my parents and others who hold rightful positions of authority.

_____ 5. I take care of my body and treat others with kindness as well.

_____ 6. I treat my sexuality and that of other people with respect and dignity.

_____ 7. I don't steal or cheat.

_____ 8. I don't lie, gossip, or spread rumors.

_____ 9. I control my sexual thoughts.

_____ 10. I am not jealous of others' possessions, and I try not to be materialistic.

3. *Entry into the Promised Land (c. 1200 B.C.):* After freeing the Chosen People from slavery in Egypt, Yahweh gave them a new and fertile land. Joshua, taking over leadership of the people from Moses, led the Israelites across the Jordan River into the land of Canaan. There the Israelites settled on the mountainsides with their cattle, sheep and goats, and gradually captured the surrounding Canaanite villages and towns.

4. *Creation of a monarchy (c. 1020 B.C.):* Not too long before 1000 B.C. the enterprising Israelites became strong enough to set up their own government. Saul, their first king, led them to victory against the Canaanites and other neighboring tribes. King David, his successor, captured the important city of Jerusalem and built his palace there. David gained the admiration and respect of the neighboring nations. He became the symbol of military might and glory. Later generations looked to his rule as the golden age of Jewish political power.

After David's son Solomon built the first Temple, Jewish political power declined. From around 922 B.C., when the country was split into the northern kingdom of Israel and the southern kingdom of Judah, the Chosen People yearned for a unified nation under a strong leader. Their hopes centered on the prophecies concerning a leader-king, or Messiah, who would re-establish the Jews as a strong, peaceful nation. They based their hopes on Yahweh's promise to send a Messiah who would establish his kingdom on earth.

Read Jos 3 and 6.

Describe two miracles Yahweh performed for the Jews at the time they entered the Holy Land.

When Jesus entered Jerusalem toward the end of his ministry, the people proclaimed their faith in him:

> *Hosanna* to the son of David!
> *Blessed is he who is coming in the name of the Lord!*
>   (Mt 21:9).

Read 2 Sam 7:8-16.

What does Yahweh promise in these verses?

This outpouring of faith showed that the people believed that Jesus was the promised Messiah.

▪ *journal* ▪

The Jews believe that King David composed the psalms. Prayerfully read Psalm 103. Write out several of your favorite lines from this psalm in your journal.

5. *Fall of the northern kingdom to the Assyrians (722 B.C.):*   The divided kingdom soon became prey to the enemies of the Israelites. The northern kingdom suffered internal strife with resulting changes in dynasty. Finally, in 722 B.C., Assyria, its mighty eastern neighbor, conquered it. Most of its people resettled in Mesopotamia, where they were soon absorbed by the Assyrians.

When the Assyrians overran the northern kingdom, they left behind the crippled, the blind, the sick, the elderly and a few who were able to hide. Emigrants from Assyria intermarried with these remnant Jews. These people became known as Samaritans, named for Samaria, the chief city of the region. The Samaritans adopted pagan customs and only gradually returned to the worship of the one true God. When the Jews returned, they did not allow the Samaritans to worship in Jerusalem, so the Samaritans erected their own shrine on the mountain Gerizim. Hostility festered between the two groups, who became hated enemies. The pious Jew of Jesus' day would not dare associate with them.

6. *Promises amidst woe: the role of the prophets.*   During this time of strife, Yahweh sent great prophets like Isaiah, Jeremiah, Hosea and Ezekiel. They interpreted what was happening to the Chosen People and why. Yahweh wanted his Chosen People to uphold their part of the covenant. Even though the people time and again wandered away from God, the story of the Hebrew Scriptures tells us that

Yahweh always remained faithful. The prophets' task was to remind the people of this, even if at times they spoke harshly of God's feeling for them.

Jeremiah spoke in strong terms, comparing God's people to a harlot who had abandoned him. Hosea spoke of Yahweh's justice in punishing an unfaithful Israel, an Israel that had fallen into the worship of false gods (idolatry). However, Hosea also proclaimed Yahweh's faithful, passionate love for his beloved, Israel. Yahweh would never abandon the people. This was the promise of the covenant.

Even though the Jews suffered because of their failure to live up to the covenant, the prophets always kept alive the message of hope and salvation. They proclaimed that one day God would establish his rule of peace and justice. This would happen through a Chosen One of God, someone who would redeem the people and rule on David's throne.

7. *Southern kingdom falls and the exile (587-537 B.C.)*:   For a while, the southern kingdom fared better than the northern, but in 587 B.C. the Babylonian king Nebuchadnezzar captured Jerusalem. This event began the period known as the Babylonian Captivity, a low point in Jewish national history. The invaders deported most able-bodied people to Babylonia. The Chosen People survived there because the Babylonians treated them relatively well and allowed them to practice their religion and to maintain a separate ethnic identity.

The prophet Ezekiel and the writer-prophet known as Second Isaiah promised on behalf of Yahweh that the Chosen People would eventually return to the Promised Land:

> Do not be afraid, for I am with you.
> I shall bring your offspring from the east,
> and gather you from the west.
> To the north I shall say, "Give them up!"
> and to the south, "Do not hold them back!" (Is 43:5-6).

In 538 B.C., Cyrus of Persia overran Babylonia. He permitted captured peoples to return to their homelands. Many of those who considered the southern kingdom of Judah their home did return. A large number probably remained along the Tigris and Euphrates rivers because the soil was more fertile there. Since those who returned to Palestine were nearly all people whose parents and grandparents came from Judah, the group became known as Jews.

The Suffering Servant

The author of Second Isaiah encouraged his exiled brothers and sisters to remain faithful to the Law. His writings promised that God would eventually redeem the Chosen People from their sufferings. Yahweh would raise up a servant whose sufferings would win salvation for them.

The writings of this prophet were very important to Jesus. Jesus studied and prayed over the prophets and discovered in them a description of his own ministry of service. Please read Isaiah 52:13-53:12 (the "Suffering Servant Song"). List three points from this passage that apply to Jesus' life.

1.

2.

3.

8. *Return, rebuilding of the temple and renewal of the covenant (537-428 B.C.):*   Under the new leader Zerubbabel and two prophets, Haggai and Zechariah, the Temple was rebuilt in Jerusalem (520-516 B.C.). The Jews were still having trouble with the Samaritans and other neighbors. Jerusalem still lay in ruins. However, Nehemiah rebuilt the city, and Ezra, a priest and scribe, restored and renewed the ancient religion.

Palestine was relatively peaceful under the Persians. This lasted for about 200 years until Alexander the Great conquered this part of the world. In the midst of this new turmoil, the Jews remained strong in their conviction that a Messiah-king would reestablish their former political glory. They held firm to the prophecy of Jeremiah who wrote during the exile that Yahweh would establish a new covenant:

"Look, the days are coming, Yahweh declares, when
I shall make a new covenant with the House of Israel
(and the House of Judah). . . . Within them I shall
plant my Law, writing it on their hearts. Then I shall
be their God and they will be my people. . . . [T]hey
will all know me . . . since I shall forgive their guilt
and never more call their sin to mind" (Jer 31:31-34).

9. *Tribulations under the Greeks (332-175 B.C.):*   In 332
B.C., the dashing Alexander the Great conquered Palestine,
bringing with him Greek culture and thought. His successors, the Ptolemies of Egypt, exiled many Jews to Egypt.
In general, the Jews prospered under this new regime,
though they had to pay exorbitant taxes.

The Seleucids of Syria succeeded the Ptolemies. The
worst of these rulers was Antiochus IV who hated the Jews
and treated them as dangerous enemies. He attacked Jerusalem on the Sabbath, knowing that the true believers
would refuse to fight on that day. He gave orders that
Greek gods be worshipped. Antiochus banned the Torah
and destroyed copies of Hebrew scriptures. He also put to
death anyone who observed the Sabbath, circumcised their
sons or refused to eat pork. In December of 168 B.C. the
worst crime of all took place. Antiochus splattered the sanc-
tuary of the Temple with the blood of a swine and rede-
dicated it to the pagan god, Zeus. To the Jews this was an
"appalling abomination" (Dn 11:31). Many Jews chose to
die than to abandon their worship of the one true God.

10. *The Maccabean revolt and Hasmonean rule (164-63
B.C.):*   Despite all the political oppression outlined above,
the Jews always enjoyed some type of religious freedom
until the hated Antiochus came along. In reaction to him,
the Maccabeus family under the brilliant Judas commanded
a revolt which eventually led to Jewish self-rule for almost
a century. Thus began the Hasmonean Dynasty (so-named
after the Maccabeus family's original tribal surname). For
the first time since the southern kingdom fell, over 400
years earlier, the Chosen People had self-rule.

This new dynasty extended its power throughout the
lands once held by King David and his son Solomon.
Unfortunately, the new kings fell victim to the vices of

many secular rulers: political intrigue, suspicion, murders, inter-family quarrels. This led to civil war. Eventually the political instability opened the way for a strong enemy: Rome. The Chosen People would not control Palestine again until 1948, when the new state of Israel was established.

11. *Roman rule (63 B.C.-lifetime of the Savior)*:   The Hasmonean rule ended when the Roman general Pompey captured Jerusalem in 63 B.C. The Romans controlled the area of Palestine for several centuries after Pompey's victory. During the rule of this last oppressor, the Romans, Jesus was born.

Throughout his public ministry, Jesus must have seen many Roman soldiers. Many of his fellow Jews despised the Romans because they believed only Yahweh had the right to rule God's Chosen People.

Rome did give Jews some privileges, for example, not conscripting Jews into the army and, most important, allowing the Jews to worship Yahweh as they wished, as long as they didn't pose a threat to the emperor. Rome also allowed each community in Palestine to have its own coun-

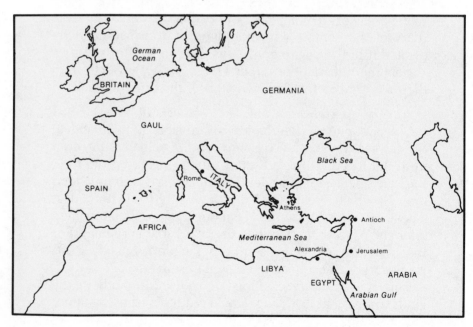

cil. In Judea the Sanhedrin, or Great Council, could make various laws, administer justice and interpret religious matters, though Rome reserved the right to inflict the death penalty.

Rome, however, carefully controlled the selection of the high priest, the most influential political/religious office permitted the Jews. The high priest was largely a puppet of the Roman procurators.

The average Jew of Jesus' day hated the Romans. Jewish subjects despised paying these taxes. They believed that this tax money belonged to God and should be spent for religious purposes like support of the Temple. The right to collect the tax went to the highest bidder. Most of the tax collectors, called publicans, abused their power through bribes and exorbitant rates. Everyone despised publicans; they were considered the same as robbers and no better than prostitutes. Imagine the shock Jesus caused when he associated with these hated men.

Rome allowed Herod the Great's son, Herod Antipas, to rule Galilee and Perea (Transjordan) throughout Jesus' youth and during his public ministry. The New Testament tells us that he spied on Jesus. Jesus called him a fox when some Pharisees warned Jesus that Herod was plotting against him. As a Galilean, Jesus was under Herod's jurisdiction.

Like his father, Herod Antipas was a builder. He constructed the new city of Tiberias on the western shore of the Sea of Galilee. He named it after the emperor to gain favor with him.

The Jews disliked Herod Antipas, especially after he divorced his wife to marry Herodias, his niece and wife of his half-brother. He executed John the Baptist for criticizing this marriage. The emperor eventually exiled him to Gaul in A.D. 39.

The Roman leader who figured most prominently in Jesus' life was Pontius Pilate. Pilate was the fifth Roman prefect to rule in Samaria, Judea and Idumea after Rome deposed Herod the Great's cruel, bloodthirsty son, Archelaus, in A.D.6. Pilate was directly answerable to the governor of Syria; he ruled from A.D. 26-36.

Pilate's headquarters were on the coast at Caesarea, but he came to Jerusalem for the great Jewish feasts. He brought his army along to discourage any possible Jewish rebellion. Under Roman law, only he had the power to execute criminals.

The Jews hated Pilate. He was a symbol of all that was wrong about Roman occupation. Philo, a Jewish contemporary of Pilate, wrote that his rule was dominated by:

> briberies, insults, robberies, outrages and wanton injuries, executions without trial constantly repeated, ceaseless and supremely grievous cruelty.

Eventually, Pilate was recalled to Rome and exiled to Gaul.

Religious Groups in Jesus' Day

Jesus did not operate in a religious vacuum. Several religious groups within Judaism vied for the attention of the Jewish people. Each stressed certain beliefs and practices that they thought were important for living out God's will. All of them were faithful Jews with good intentions but at times their ideas about the best way to live their faith conflicted with Jesus' teaching.

Zealots.   The Zealots do not figure prominently in the gospels. They appear only in connection with one of Jesus' apostles, Simon the Zealot.

The Zealots were very anxious for the coming of God's kingdom. Unlike Jesus, however, they believed that the kingdom could only come if the Messiah would lead a rebellion against the Romans. They hated the Romans and disliked any group of Jews—like the Sadducees—that helped the Romans. They believed only Yahweh should be honored as king or Lord. They abhorred paying taxes to a foreign emperor.

Their center of operations was Galilee, Jesus' own home district. He probably knew many Zealots. They would have urged Jesus to become a political messiah, a military figure who would use violence to gain freedom for the Jews. Galilee was a hotbed of rebel activity, and there were several false messiahs who tried to foment revolution even in Jesus' lifetime. The Zealot movement eventually led to the First Jewish Revolt or holy war against Rome which took place between A.D. 66-70. This revolt led to the destruction of the Temple in A.D. 70.

Jesus was opposed to the aims of this group. He taught his followers to love their enemies and turn the other cheek in the face of violence.

Essenes.   The Jewish historian Josephus wrote about the Zealots and also the Essenes. We did not know much about the Essenes until the discovery of the Dead Sea Scrolls, which reveal much about their teachings and lifestyle.

Many of the Essenes lived in the desert in a monastic community at Qumran on the northwest shore of the Dead Sea. They lived a rigorous life. Most did not marry. They shared goods in common. Founded by a "Teacher of Righteousness" sometime during the Maccabean era, they rejected the official priestly leaders in Jerusalem. They believed that the last days were fast approaching.

The Essenes divided all of reality into the Sons of Light, representing truth, and the Sons of Darkness, led by an Angel of Darkness. According to them, the battle between these two spiritual realities is waged in each person as well. Eventually God will win the battle. According to the Essenes, two messiahs will bring about God's victory. The first will be a kingly messiah descended from David. The second will be a priestly messiah even more important than the kingly one.

Jesus would have known of their existence. Some scholars even suggest that John the Baptist might at one time have been one of their members since they were known for their ritual washings. John baptized in the Jordan near the Qumran community.

The Romans destroyed the Essenes around A.D. 70 during the First Jewish Revolt. Though there are some similarities between this sect and Jesus, there are major differences as well. For example, the Essenes instructed their members to hate their enemies; Jesus taught love instead. The Essenes required vigorous discipline that only the highly motivated could endure; Jesus' message was open to all people.

Pharisees.   The Pharisees, an influential lay movement popular in the towns, desired to follow God by living the Law (Torah) as perfectly as they could. This was a praise-worthy aim. To accomplish it, their leaders taught many customs (known as the "oral law") to regulate every aspect of daily life. Keeping these customs reminded the Pharisees that they could find God in every area of life.

Jesus shared many beliefs with the Pharisees and was closer to them than to any other religious group of his day. However, he criticized the Pharisees' negative judgments of other Jews who did not keep all their traditions.

Jesus' idea of holiness was different from theirs. For example, the Pharisees emphasized a ritual of washing their hands before a meal. Jesus did not believe this made them holy. He taught that inner attitude is more important than external rituals.

A real danger for anyone trying to live a holy life is the temptation to pride. Jesus detected this vice in the way some Pharisees believed they were better and more holy than other people, and he criticized them for it.

Not all the Pharisees of Jesus' day were narrow-minded and judgmental. Two outstanding and influential Pharisees were the scholars Shammai and Hillel. A disciple of Jesus, Nicodemus, was a Pharisee, and St. Paul was a famous Pharisee before his conversion to Jesus.

Sadducees.   The Sadducees made up a small but power-ful religious group. Taking their name from Sadok, a high priest from the days of King Solomon, the Sadducees were from priestly, wealthy and aristocratic families. They were centered in Jerusalem and focused on Temple worship.

Sadducees were part of "The Establishment." They believed in pleasing and cooperating with Roman occupa-tion. Many of them held positions in the Sanhedrin, the leading ruling body of the Jews in Jerusalem. They gave Jesus to Pilate in large part because they feared the Romans might turn on the Jewish people because of Jesus' popu-larity with the crowds.

A good way to study the Pharisees and Sadducees is through a comparison of their beliefs. Note how they con-flict or agree with Jesus and with one another.

SADDUCEES	PHARISEES	JESUS
Accepted only the first 5 books of the Old Testament as inspired	Accepted the Torah, the Prophets, and Other Writings, plus their own oral traditions, as God's word	Accepted the Hebrew scriptures, but interpreted them in an original way
Denied the doctrine of the resurrection of the body	Accepted the doctrine of the resurrection of the body	Believed in the resurrection: "I am the resurrection" (Jn 11:25)
Denied that angels exist	Believed in angels	Believed in angels
Strict code of justice: "Eye for eye, tooth for tooth."	More liberal code of justice. Hillel taught: "What is hateful to you, do not do it unto your neighbor."	Taught love of enemy and the Golden Rule: "So always treat others as you would like them to treat you" (Mt 7:12)
Strong emphasis on human freedom	Strong emphasis on God's control over human affairs	Strong emphasis on a caring, loving God who wants us to use freedom properly
Cooperated with the Romans	Hated the Romans	Forgave his enemies and taught respect for everyone

Jesus and Religious Groups

1. Read Jesus' public debate with the Sadducees in Matthew 22:23-33. Answer the following questions:

   a. What case did the Sadducees pose to Jesus?

   b. How did Jesus answer it?

   c. How did he prove that the first five books of the scriptures, the Torah taught by Moses, demonstrated a belief in the resurrection?

2. Read what Jesus had to say about some of the Pharisees and scribes in Matthew 23. List three charges Jesus brings against them:

   a.

   b.

   c.

▪ discuss ▪

From the chart on the preceding page, compare Jesus' teaching of the Golden Rule with Hillel's summary of the Law. How are they different? How are they the same?

▪ summary ▪

1. To understand Jesus, we need to appreciate the story of God's Chosen People, our ancestors in the faith. The story begins when God called Abraham and formed a *covenant* with him, promising that he would bless him with descendants. Abraham responded to God in faith.

2. The Exodus is the great event in Jewish history. With Yahweh's direction, Moses led his people from slavery in Egypt through the desert to a new land. Yahweh gave his people the Ten Commandments. By living these commandments, the Chosen People were to show other nations the way to the one true God.

3. Joshua crossed the Jordan River and led God's people into the Promised Land. After some time, God raised up King David to lead his people. Jesus' contemporaries looked on David's and his son Solomon's reigns as the Golden Age. They expected a Messiah who would reestablish Israel's ancient glory.

4. The story of God's people shows that God was always merciful and faithful to his promises, even when the Chosen People sinned and forgot God's promises. Great prophets like Jeremiah, Isaiah, Hosea and Ezekiel reminded the Jews of their vocation and warned of God's punishments.

5. Major tragedies which befell the Chosen People included the fall of the northern kingdom in 722 B.C., the fall of the southern kingdom in 587 B.C. and Exile in Babylon between 587-537 B.C.

6. God allowed the Chosen People to return to the Promised Land in 537 B.C. They rebuilt the Temple and reestablished their religion. They continued to hope for a Messiah who would restore them to their former glory.

7. The Greeks under Alexander the Great conquered Palestine in 322 B.C. The worst of Alexander's successors was Antiochus IV who hated the Jews and forbade them to worship as God's people. Finally, the Jews revolted against this cruel ruler under the Maccabean family. The Chosen People had their independence until Rome conquered Palestine in 63 B.C.

8. The two prominent leaders during Jesus' public life were Herod Antipas and Pontius Pilate. Herod spied on Jesus' activities and executed John the Baptist. The Roman prefect Pontius Pilate was a vindictive ruler who eventually crucified Jesus.

9. There were four prominent religious groups in Jesus day. The Zealots advocated a violent overthrow of Roman rule. The Essenes lived a strict, communal life; they expected both a kingly messiah and priestly messiah. The Sadducees cooperated with the Romans. They controlled the Sanhedrin, the official Jewish ruling body, and centered their authority on Temple worship. The

Pharisees tried to live the Law strictly. They had much influence over the people. Jesus criticized their pride and the oral traditions they added to the written law.

· *focus questions* ·

1. Identify the following:

    Major Jewish figures

    Abraham
    Moses
    Joshua
    David
    Solomon
    Jeremiah
    Isaiah
    Hosea
    Ezekiel
    Zerubbabel
    Haggai and Zechariah
    Nehemiah and Ezra
    the Maccabees

    Enemies of the Jews

    Nebuchadnezzar
    Cyrus of Persia
    Alexander the
    Great
    Antiochus IV
    Pompey
    Herod Antipas
    Pontius Pilate

    Significant Events/Concepts

    covenant
    Exodus experience/Passover
    Babylonian Captivity
    Sanhedrin

2. Who were the Samaritans? Why were they and the Jews enemies?

3. When did the Chosen People get the name Jews?

4. What was the so-called "disastrous abomination"?

5. Describe what Jewish life was like under the Romans.

6. Why were publicans hated by the average Jew in Jesus' time? What was Jesus' attitude toward them?

7. Discuss two beliefs of each of the following groups:

    a. Zealots   b. Essenes
    c. Sadducees   d. Pharisees

8. When did the First Jewish Revolt take place? Name two of its effects.

▪ *journal entries* ▪

1. Consult a bible atlas. Find the Holy Land in relationship to the Roman Empire's other provinces. Answer the following in your journal: In what way was Palestine insignificant and yet very important? Why do you suppose this area has changed hands so many times during history? Why is this area so important to today's history?

2. Read Luke 7:36-50. Answer the following questions in your journal.

   a. Give evidence that Simon the Pharisee invited Jesus to dinner only to test him.

   b. What is the point of the parable that Jesus told at the dinner table?

   c. What saved the woman?

   Pretend that you are the woman Jesus forgave. Write what you would tell your family and friends about Jesus. Mention your feelings. Describe what it means for Jesus to forgive *you*.

3. *Enriching your vocabulary.*   Using a good dictionary, look up the meaning of the following words. Write the definitions in your journal.

abomination	fester
abhor	foment
conscript	oppressor
emigrant	patriarch
exorbitant	remnant

Prayer Reflection

You must love Yahweh your God with all your heart, with all your soul, with all your strength.
—Deuteronomy 6:5

The greatest Jewish prayer is the *shema* (from the Hebrew word for *hear* or *listen*), a prayer pious Jews recite daily. This prayer reminds the Chosen People, and us, their spiritual descendants, what is most important in this life. This is the first prayer every Jewish child learns; it is the last thing every dying Jew hopes to have on his or her lips.

> "Listen, Israel: Yahweh our God is the one, the only Yahweh. You must love Yahweh your God with all your heart, with all your soul, with all your strength"(Dt 6:4-5).

▪ *reflection* ▪

Do you love God above everything else? How do you show it?

▪ *resolution* ▪

Think of one thing in your life that prevents you from loving God more. Resolve to begin to correct it this week.

chapter 5

Jesus

The Teacher

"Listen, a sower went out to sow. As he sowed, some seeds fell on the edge of the path, and the birds came and ate them up. Others fell on patches of rock where they found little soil and sprang up at once, because there was no depth of earth; but as soon as the sun came up they were scorched and, not having any roots, they withered away. Others fell among thorns, and the thorns grew up and choked them. Others fell on rich soil and produced their crop, some a hundred-fold, some sixty, some thirty. Anyone who has ears should listen!"

—Matthew 13:4-9

In This Chapter

We will look at:

- Jesus' teaching style
- parables
- a summary of Jesus' message

Bumper stickers amuse us because they often capture truth in a few words. Every teacher likes the one that reads: "If you can read this, thank a teacher."

Jesus was an extraordinary teacher. The New Testament tells us that friend and foe addressed Jesus as *rabbi*, the Hebrew word for "teacher." He was so popular with the people that it upset his opponents. What made Jesus such an appealing teacher?

Jesus was remarkable because of the message he delivered and the way he delivered it. Henry Brooke Adams once remarked: "A teacher affects eternity; he can never tell where his influence stops." Jesus personifies this statement. His message has eternal significance.

When we hear, reflect, understand and put into practice Jesus' teachings, we will have much to thank him for.

Living Jesus' Teaching

The Sermon on the Mount, Matthew 5—7, contains a masterful summary of Jesus' teaching on how to live. Jesus does not want his followers simply to *know* his teaching, but rather to put it into practice.

Reflect on these words from the Sermon on the Mount. Judge how well you actually live this teaching.

+ — I take this teaching to heart and really live it.
? — I haven't thought that much about this.
0 — I know I should be living this, but I often fail to put it into practice.

_____ 1. "Anyone who is angry with a brother will answer for it" (5:22).

_____ 2. "Do not swear at all" (5:34).

_____ 3. "Love your enemies and pray for those who persecute you" (5:44).

_____ 4. "Be careful not to parade your uprightness in public to attract attention" (6:1).

_____ 5. "Do not store up treasures for yourselves on earth, where moth and woodworm destroy them and thieves can break in and steal" (6:19).

_____ 6. "You cannot be the slave both of God and of money" (6:24).

_____ 7. "So do not worry about tomorrow: tomorrow will take care of itself. Each day has enough trouble of its own" (6:34).

_____ 8. "Do not judge, and you will not be judged" (7:1).

_____ 9. "Ask, and it will be given to you; search, and you will find; knock, and the door will be opened to you" (7:7).

_____ 10. "So always treat others as you would like them to treat you" (7:12).

▪ *discuss* ▪

1. What is swearing? List some situations that make people want to do it. How can we avoid it?

2. Who are your enemies? How do they become enemies? How can we pray for them?

3. Discuss how money and material possessions enslave us. What role does advertising play in selling a materialistic lifestyle? Give examples.

4. List the 10 most common worries you and your classmates may have. Why is each one a problem? What can be done about them? Can worry help at all? Explain.

Jesus' Teaching Style

Read the entire Sermon on the Mount, Mt 5—7. Pick out three of your favorite teachings. List them in your journal and write a paragraph on each telling specifically how you can apply them to your life.

Jesus' message itself is life-giving, but Jesus was also an exceptional teacher—easy to listen to and a good person to be around. Even today when we read the New Testament his voice echoes down the centuries and touches our hearts. What made him such an outstanding teacher? Let's look at some characteristics of his teaching style.

Jesus Was in Touch With People.   Jesus instructed more by his deeds than by his words. He was genuine. For example, he taught that the highest love we can show is to lay down our lives for others, and he himself freely gave up his life for us.

Jesus went after people. He did not wait for them to come to him. He was a wandering preacher and teacher who taught everywhere—on hillsides, on dusty roads, at the tables of the rich and poor, in synagogues and in the Temple, on the seashore and in the marketplace. He taught wherever people were willing to hear the good news. He attracted their interest, held their attention and inspired their loyalty.

Jesus loved life and related to people on their level. He performed his first miracle while enjoying himself at a wedding feast. Jesus loved to eat and drink, so much that his enemies accused him of being a glutton and a drunk.

Jesus Used Colorful, Down-to-Earth Language.   His language was picturesque. Jesus' metaphors and similes create vibrant images that make us think and take notice. For example, Jesus told us that the Son of man will come very quickly.

"[T]he coming of the Son of man will be like lightning striking in the east and flashing far into the west.

> Wherever the corpse is, that is where the vultures will gather" (Mt 24:27-28).

Jesus used graphic images to inform us of our vocation:

> "You are salt for the earth. But if salt loses its taste, what can make it salty again? It is good for nothing, and can only be thrown out to be trampled under people's feet.
> "You are light for the world" (Mt 5:13-14).

Jesus used *hyperbole*, or exaggeration, to make a point. You might be familiar with this statement: "This exam is going to kill me." Hyperbole drives home a point, but we should not take it literally. Jesus said,

> "If your right eye should be your downfall, tear it out and throw it away. . . . And if your right hand should be your downfall, cut it off and throw it away; for it will do you less harm to lose one part of yourself than to have your whole body go to hell" (Mt 5:29-30).

He stresses the need to resist temptation rather than risk hell. He does not want us to mutilate ourselves.

Jesus Spoke With Authority. Rabbis of Jesus' day typically quoted prominent teachers to back up their positions. Jesus quoted no other rabbi, and when he quoted scriptures, he gave novel, penetrating and profound interpretations of what he saw there.

We can see authority in the way Jesus used the simple word *Amen*, a Hebrew word that means "certainly." It was always used at the end of an oath or a blessing or a curse and showed agreement. Jesus used this simple word to introduce and to strengthen his own words, "Amen, amen, I say. . . ."

Jesus Was a Brilliant Debater. Jesus' opponents often tried to trap him in one of his own teachings, but Jesus would have none of their games. One example involves the coin of tribute Jews were expected to give to the Roman emperor. Pious Jews hated paying it. One day the Pharisees approached Jesus with the question, "Is it permissible to pay taxes to Caesar or not?" (Mt 22:17). If Jesus said no, his opponents would claim he was preaching rebellion against Rome, a crime punishable by death. If he said yes, he would lose face with zealous Jews who hated the Roman tax. Jesus understood clearly the malice of the question. He asked his opponents to show him a coin, a clever move because his opponents should not have been carrying a Roman coin if they hated the Romans as much as they claimed. Their hypocrisy was immediately clear. Jesus' responded:

> "Very well, pay Caesar what belongs to Caesar—and God what belongs to God." When they heard this they were amazed; they left him alone and went away (Mt 22:21-22).

Jesus Challenges Us. Good teachers stretch their students' minds; they challenge their students to grow. When the rich aristocrat asked Jesus what he must do to gain eternal life, Jesus reviewed the commandments with him. When the man assured Jesus that he had kept all the commandments, Jesus challenged him to sell everything he owned, distribute his money to the poor, and come follow him. The gospel challenges us to examine our consciences.

Jesus the Teacher

Jesus used thought-provoking paradox in his teaching. Often this took the form of short, memorable sayings of great significance. Memorize the following quotes. Then discuss the meaning of each.

> "Anyone who wants to save his life will lose it; but anyone who loses his life for my sake, will save it" (Lk 9:24).

> "The least among you all is the one who is the greatest" (Lk 9:48).

> "For everyone who raises himself up will be humbled, and the one who humbles himself will be raised up" (Lk 14:11).

▪ *journal* ▪

Please read the following passages and discuss in your journal how Jesus showed his debating ability:

the woman caught in adultery (Jn 8:1-11)

the traditions of Pharisees violate the intent of the Law (Mk 7:1-23)

Jesus defends his authority to teach (Mt 21:23-27)

▪ *discuss* ▪

As a class, list 10 traits of an ideal teacher. Discuss how Jesus fits your description. Try to find examples from the gospels to support your answers.

Parables

Jesus was a storyteller. He told simple, vivid stories drawn from ordinary life that convey religious truth. Jesus used such parables because stories convey truth in a more interesting, memorable way than merely teaching facts. Jesus' disciples did not take notes. People in Jesus' day had to remember what a teacher taught. Jesus' stories were so vivid that his listeners could easily recall them.

For example, read the story of Lazarus and the rich man (Lk 16:19-31). Through this story Jesus warns that the wealthy must share their riches with the poor or God will punish them in eternity. Instead of simply telling people this, Jesus tells about Lazarus, so poor and sick that he longed to eat scraps from the rich man's table, although the rich man himself never noticed Lazarus.

Before long, the two men died. The rich man was buried and went to hell, where he suffered every torment. He saw a vision of Lazarus in heaven, totally happy with Abraham. The rich man begged Abraham to allow Lazarus to dip the tip of his finger in water to cool his tongue for he was in agony burning in the flames. Abraham refused the rich man his request. Nor could Lazarus appear to his five brothers to warn them what was in store for them if they didn't change their selfish ways.

How could anyone forget this story once they heard it? How could they forget the message Jesus was teaching?

Parables also enable people to take a fresh look at reality. To understand what Jesus is saying, people must be willing to let go of their preconceptions. Parables compare something familiar—seeds, wheat, yeast, sheep, farmers, nets—to an unfamiliar idea about God's kingdom. Through parables, Jesus challenges us to use our imaginations and our emotions as well as our minds to grapple with the truth. A story makes us think, to feel, to find hidden layers of meaning, to probe and to reflect. Jesus tells stories that are windows into God's world.

Consider, for example, the parable of the pearl:

> "The kingdom of Heaven is like a merchant looking for fine pearls; when he finds one of great value he goes and sells everything he owns and buys it" (Mt 13:45-46).

So valuable is the pearl this man finds that he surrenders his entire fortune to buy it. The reign of God is like that. When we find it, we should stake our whole life on it.

Reading the Parables of Jesus

Below is a list of parables not discussed in this chapter.
1. Read five of these parables and write an interpretation of each in your journal.
2. Rewrite your favorite parable in a contemporary setting. Use vivid, colorful language. Share what you wrote with your classmates.

Rules for Interpreting Parables: Keep these rules in mind when interpreting the parables:

1. Figure out what the story as a story means. For example, Jesus compared the reign of God to the yeast a woman mixed in with *three* measures of flour (read Mt 13:33). "Three measures" is equal to 75 pounds—quite a bit of flour! Nonetheless, the yeast does its job and causes the dough to rise.

2. Find one major point of comparison. Scholars agree that most parables only have one point of comparison, and the emphasis is usually at the end of the story. When Jesus was asked "Who is my neighbor?" (Lk 10:29), he told the story of the Good Samaritan. The Samaritan who helped the victim of banditry was an enemy. Thus, our neighbor is everyone, even our enemies.

3. Refer to a bible commentary. Countless books discuss the meaning of each book of the Bible. Check your school or local library for some of these commentaries. Trained scripture scholars help show us what Jesus means by his teaching.

Parables of Jesus	Matthew	Mark	Luke
The great dinner	22:1-14		14:15-24
The wicked workers	21:33-46	12:1-2	20:9-19
The Pharisee and the tax collector			18:9-14
The wise and foolish maidens	25:1-13		
The pounds and talents	25:14-30		19:11-27
The unforgiving servant	18:23-35		

Summary of Jesus' Teaching

Let us now turn to the content of Jesus' teaching. Below are some of his key concepts and themes.

Reign of God. Jesus immediately began to proclaim God's reign. The kingdom of God is not a place. Rather, it means God's reign over our hearts, the process of God reconciling and renewing all things through Jesus. When Jesus preached that the reign is near, he was saying that God is near. Salvation is happening now.

God's people awaited the day when Yahweh's justice would become a reality. They expected that the Promised One would bring Yahweh's peace to the land, justice to the poor, comfort to widows and orphans and usher in God's reign. Jesus did just that.

Jesus spoke about the reign of God in images. It starts small like a mustard seed, but it will grow large. It spreads in its own mysterious way, like yeast working in dough or seeds secretly growing in the earth. Its harvest will be greater than we can possibly imagine.

Forgiveness.   Jesus proclaims forgiveness and mercy. He associated with all kinds of people, especially those who needed God's love and forgiveness: tax collectors, the poor, prostitutes, the sick, "losers." When self-righteous people criticized Jesus for associating with these outcasts, he replied:

> "It is not the healthy who need the doctor, but the sick. I came to call not the upright, but sinners" (Mk 2:17).

On one occasion when the Pharisees and scribes complained about Jesus' association with sinners, Jesus told three important parables of forgiveness: the lost sheep, the lost coin and the prodigal son. The point of these parables is that God loves us so much that he will go to every extreme to show his love. His love, especially for the lost sinner, goes beyond what we can comprehend.

Abba.   Jesus reveals that God is like a father who wants to come close to his children. God wants us to seek and do his will. God will always love us. When Jesus addressed God in prayer, he used the Aramaic word *Abba*, or daddy, a term of endearment. This word reveals the heart of the gospel.

Read Luke 13:18-19
parables of the reign of God

Read Luke 15
stories of God's mercy and forgiveness

Read Luke 11:1-13
the Lord's Prayer

When Jesus' contemporaries prayed, they used terms of great respect, such as "Master of Heaven and Earth," that emphasized God's divinity and superiority over creation. Jesus invites his followers to address God as Abba when he teaches us the Lord's Prayer, revealing an earth-shaking truth: *The almighty God is our loving Father, an intimate daddy who will care for us and love us.*

Jesus tells us God will give us what is good for us, just as human parents do:

> "Ask, and it will be given to you; search, and you will find; knock, and the door will be opened to you" (Lk 11:9).

Love and Forgiveness

Not everyone sees love and forgiveness the way Jesus does. Here are some other views. Mark what you believe about them according to this scale: 1 — strongly agree; 2 — agree; 3 — don't know; 4 — disagree; 5 —strongly disagree.

_____ 1. We should forgive only when someone is truly sorry.

_____ 2. "Love means never having to say you are sorry." (The film *Love Story*)

_____ 3. The greatest sign of love is forgiveness—with no strings attached.

_____ 4. "Good to forgive; best to forget!" —Robert Browning

_____ 5. One of the hardest things to say is "I'm sorry."

_____ 6. "Love is love's reward." —John Dryden

_____ 7. "Blessed are the merciful" (Mt 5:7).

▪ *discuss* ▪

1. List ways we express sorrow and forgiveness to each other (for example, an embrace, a gift, a kind word). How do you show sorrow to others for something you have done?

2. List and discuss ten actions or failures to act for which young people should ask God's forgiveness.

· *journal* ·

Using a contemporary setting, rewrite the parable of the Prodigal Son. Write it in the first person as a wayward or faithful son or daughter. Be sure to express your feelings about your father's actions and words.

Salvation. Jesus emphasized that a new age had dawned, that the day of salvation had arrived. He spoke of new wine being poured into new wineskins, of a new harvest, of the need to put on new robes. His vivid image of a wedding feast, a familiar symbol for Jews of heaven and God's presence among his people, especially announces that the Lord is among his people.

Jesus came to assure us that salvation is taking place. Christians believe that Jesus is the savior of all people. God gives it as he pleases, just like the landowner dispensed wages freely and generously to workers who only labored for an hour.

Salvation comes through repentance and forgiveness of sin. In speaking to the wealthy tax collector Zacchaeus, Jesus says:

> "Today salvation has come to this house, . . . for the Son of man has come to seek out and save what was lost" (Lk 19:9-10).

Jesus demonstrated that he is the Savior by performing many miracles, signs of God's power. They show the reality of the good news. The gospels of Matthew, Mark and Luke use the word *save* to show healing accomplished by Jesus. Jesus brings the healing of salvation.

Faith and Repentance. When Jesus announces the reign of God, he challenges people to "Repent, and believe the gospel" (Mk 1:15). These words go together: repent and believe, faith and a change in our lives. Because God's reign is now, we should repent, that is, change our lives. Then we should believe the good news of salvation.

Read Luke 14:15-24
the reign of God is like
a wedding banquet
and Matthew 20:1-16
the generosity of God's salvation

Read Matthew 21:28-32
doing God's will

Change the way you are doing things. Jesus is here. Life and reality are radically different. Stop living selfishly and bitterly toward one another. God's justice is breaking into our world.

Read Matthew 7:24-27
those who hear the word of God
and act on it
and Matthew 25:31-46
whatever you do for the least
of these . . .

Love and Judgment.   The reign of God demands action. We can help the cause of salvation by being instruments of God's mercy. Love must accompany faith. Jesus came to change lives, not just to preach a message. He wants us to respond to him and to his message with our lives. Jesus said:

> "It is not anyone who says to me, 'Lord, Lord,' who will enter the kingdom of Heaven, but the person who does the will of my Father in heaven" (Mt 7:21).

Faith is necessary, but it must be built on the rock-solid foundation of loving actions.

Jesus tells us that to become his disciple, we must commit ourselves to service. Following him demands sacrifice and commitment. It means service.

> "If anyone wants to be a follower of mine, let him renounce himself and take up his cross and follow me" (Mk 8:34).

> "Anyone who wants to become great among you must be your servant, and anyone who wants to be first among you must be slave to all" (Mk 10:43-44).

The mark of the reign of God is loving those who are in need.

Jesus' message is urgent. We must respond now that we have heard the good news of God's reign. We will be judged. We don't know when God will demand this accounting of our lives, so we should always be ready. God judges us according to how we respond to the least of our brothers and sisters. Our eternal reward is based on how well we live the law of love, the ethics of God's reign:

> "For I was hungry and you gave me food, I was thirsty and you gave me drink, I was a stranger and you made me welcome, lacking clothes and you clothed me, sick and you visited me, in prison and you came to see me" (Mt 25:35-36).

Read Matthew 13:44-45
the parable of the hidden treasure
and Luke 12:16-20
"This very night your life will be
required of you."

Rejoice.   The good news Jesus came to preach met resistance. Even amidst apparent setbacks in working for God's reign, we should be joyful people. We know there is suffering and evil in our world, and forces working against God's plan. But in the end things will work out.

Those who accept God's reign have found the hidden treasure. We should stake everything on it. Jesus has revealed to us God's goodness, generosity, forgiving love and salvation. Jesus announces that good triumphs over evil.

Jesus wants us to accept his good news with joy and deep conviction. We should not wait for tomorrow because it might be too late. A foolish man in one of Jesus' parables tore down his old barns and built new ones to store his riches. Unfortunately, he did not count on dying that night. The time to choose Jesus and his Father's reign is *right now.*

The Lord wants us to believe in him and his message because he needs us to spread it. We have his joy and the good news of salvation to share with others. We are instruments of his love. "Repent, believe the good news of Jesus and live his life of love — this is the message of our Savior, Jesus Christ!"

▪ *summary* ▪

1. Jesus was an outstanding teacher because he was in touch with people. He used colorful, down-to-earth examples to illustrate his teachings. Jesus spoke with authority.

2. Jesus proved to be a brilliant debater when he had to defend his teaching.

3. Jesus' teaching "afflicts the comfortable and comforts the afflicted." Through paradoxes, riddles and other challenging statements, Jesus calls his disciples to strive for greatness in pursuit of God's reign.

4. Jesus conveyed his message through parables — vivid and memorable short stories that force people to take a fresh look at reality.

5. Jesus' message can be summarized in the following themes:

a. *Reign of God*:   God's reign of peace, justice and mercy is happening right now.

b. *Forgiveness*:   The principal sign of God's reign is forgiveness, God's mercy extended to everyone.

c. *Abba*:   God is like a loving "daddy," someone who cares for us. We can approach God with confidence.

d. *Salvation*:   The healing process to overcome sin and alienation has begun through our Lord and Savior, Jesus Christ. His miracles are a sign of the reign of God.

e. *Faith and Repentance*:   Jesus' message demands a response. He wants us to believe and to repent, that is, to change the way we live.

f. *Love and Judgment*:   Faith without good works is not enough. To believe in Jesus means we must love him by loving God above all things and our neighbor as ourselves. We will be judged on the basis of how we respond to the least of our brothers and sisters.

g. *Rejoice*:   Despite all the obstacles to God's reign, it will triumph! Christians should be joy-filled people who show the way to others.

▪ *focus questions* ▪

1. Discuss some examples of the vivid language Jesus used in his teaching.

2. What is the meaning of the word *Amen*? What does *Abba* mean? Discuss their significance in Jesus' teaching.

3. What is Jesus' position on paying taxes?

4. Discuss several reasons why Jesus spoke in parables.

5. List any three parables of Jesus. Retell the story in your own words. Interpret the meaning of each story.

6. What does the parable of the Prodigal Son mean?

7. List and discuss five key themes in Jesus' teaching. Use at least one parable to illustrate each theme.

8. Be able to explain each of the following important terms:

reign of God	repentance
parable	salvation

▪ *journal entries* ▪

1. Write an original parable to exemplify one theme in the teaching of Jesus. Use pictures from magazines or create your own artwork to illustrate your story. Be prepared to share your story with your classmates.

2. *Enriching your vocabulary.*   Using a good dictionary, look up the meaning of the following terms. Write the definitions in your journal.

desolate	paradox
grapple	prodigal
hyperbole	vibrant
lavish	

Prayer Reflection

John's gospel does not have the parables Jesus tells in the other gospels. However, according to John, Jesus does use many beautiful metaphors to help us hear the good news, such as the following:

> I am the good shepherd;
> I know my own
> and my own know me,
> just as the Father knows me
> and I know the Father;
> and I lay down my life for my sheep.

—John 10:14-15

▪ *reflection* ▪

What do you know about Jesus, the Good Shepherd? What does he know about you?

▪ *resolution* ▪

Jesus says he lays down his life for us. Name one thing you can do for him in return.

Resolve to put this into action during the coming week.

chapter 6

Jesus
A Gospel Portrait

And he said to them, "Go out to the whole world; proclaim the gospel to all creation. Whoever believes and is baptized will be saved."

—Mark 16:15-16

In This Chapter

We will look at:

- gospel formation
- Mark: The Servant Messiah
- Matthew: The New Moses
- Luke: The Savior of the World
- John: The Word of God

History remembers Napoleon Bonaparte as a small man who had monumental but momentary success in conquering Europe. He met defeat at the Battle of Waterloo and died in exile on a remote island. Historians claim Napoleon was one of the greatest generals to lead an army, yet Napoleon himself is reported to have said:

"I search in vain in history to find the similar to Jesus Christ, or anything which can approach the gospel."

Napoleon recognized that the influence of Jesus far surpassed his own, even though Jesus never led an army or held political office.

To what can we attribute Jesus' unique impact? Perhaps people follow Jesus because he *is* the good news he proclaimed. And this good news, contained in the four gospels, is as good today as it was 2,000 years ago.

We cannot get to know Jesus without knowing the gospels. St. Jerome, who first translated the Bible into Latin, said, "Ignorance of scripture is ignorance of Christ." You can find in the four gospels the answer to the three most important questions you'll ever ask: "Where did I come from? Why am I here? Where am I going?"

111

Jesus, Good News and You

Pause here to consider how you are living Jesus' message. Please rate yourself on the following statements according to the scale below:

3 — I'm making progress on this

2 — I have more setbacks than forward movement on this.

1 — I haven't given this much thought, but I should.

_____ 1. I'm making a strong effort to gain control over those things in my life that blind me to God and other people. Some examples include:

_____ a. material possessions

_____ b. harmful substances like alcohol

_____ c. peer pressure

_____ d. taking the easy way out (for example, cheating)

_____ 2. I am doing my part to help spread God's kingdom by giving my time and talents to others in need.

_____ 3. I ask for God's forgiveness when I sin, for example, by celebrating the sacrament of reconciliation.

_____ 4. I pause to think about what God has done for me personally. For example, I thank him for the many gifts he has given me.

_____ 5. I firmly believe that God loves me and cares for me.

_____ 6. I want to be a disciple of Jesus Christ and want him to be proud of me.

■ *journal* ■

Picture Jesus saying to you, "I have chosen you to do my work. Will you accept the challenge?" Write Jesus a response telling him what you feel you can do for him. If your answer is "no," explain why.

Gospel Formation

As God's inspired word, the four gospels present a timeless and reliable portrait of Jesus. The written gospels—four versions of the good news of Jesus—resulted from a gradual process of formation and composition. We can visualize the stages as:

Stage 1:	Stage 2:	Stage 3:
Historical Jesus	Oral preaching of the early church	Written gospels

Stage 1: Historical Jesus (6-4 B.C.-A.D. 30).   Jesus is the good news he came to proclaim. Through his actions, his teaching, and his death and resurrection, Jesus reveals the meaning of God's salvation. During his ministry, Jesus formed the apostles to carry on his work and teaching after his time on earth. He commissioned his disciples to teach his message, and he promised them the help of the Holy Spirit. The public ministry of Jesus lasted for about three years, A.D. 27-30. (Most scholars date the crucifixion at the 14th of the Jewish month of Nisan—our April 7—in the year 30.)

Stage 2: Oral Preaching of the Early Church (A.D. 30-65).   After Jesus' resurrection and the sending of the Holy Spirit on Pentecost, the apostles fulfilled Jesus' command to preach the good news. Remembering Jesus' teaching and inspired by the Spirit, the apostles preached the key events of Jesus' story: his sayings, his miracles, his passion and death and his resurrection. This formed the *kerygma* or core teaching about Jesus. We can find the main outlines of this preaching in several sermons given in the Acts of the Apostles.

During the period of oral preaching, the apostles were not interested in simply giving a biography of Jesus. Rather, they wanted to witness to their faith in him. But why did it take so long before anyone committed the good news to writing? First, people in those days learned by hearing and remembering. This was the method Jesus himself used. Also, early Christians believed that Jesus was coming again soon, so why bother to write out a polished, literary gospel? Perhaps around A.D. 40 or so, various collections and lists of Jesus' parables, miracles, sayings and the main outline of the passion narrative were written out to help preachers prepare sermons and recall the main points of Jesus' life and teaching.

Two major reasons led to the formal writing of the four gospels. First, eyewitnesses to Jesus' public life were dying or being martyred for their faith. Second, some misguided Christians were beginning to distort the true gospel. Thus, *to preserve authentic teaching*, the early church commissioned talented preachers to set in writing a permanent record of the good news. This written record is what we today recognize as the four gospels.

Stage 3: The Written Gospels (A.D. 65-100).   The four gospels are *authentic testimonies* concerning Jesus. They are *inspired, written, communal expressions* of the one gospel, the person of Jesus Christ. Commissioned by the early church, the evangelists composed their gospels creatively. They drew on the oral preaching and any written sources (for example, lists of the parables) available to them.

The gospels were written over a period of 35 years, from about A.D. 65-100. The four evangelists wrote for different Christian communities, and each gospel reflects (1) the needs of the original community for which it was written and (2) the creativity of the individual evangelist. For example, Luke and Mark wrote for Gentile Christians, while Matthew wrote for Jewish Christians. Mark stressed Jesus' deeds, while Luke and Matthew highlighted Jesus' parables and shorter sayings. John, on the other hand, developed a sophisticated theology on the person of Jesus.

When lined up in parallel columns, you can easily notice many similarities in Matthew, Mark and Luke. In composing their respective gospels, Matthew and Luke borrowed heavily from Mark, perhaps a version earlier than the one we have today. Matthew and Luke also drew from another common source labelled *Q* (from the German word *Quelle* which means "source"). Matthew, Mark and Luke also drew on oral and written traditions that each of them alone knew. Taken together, these three gospels are known as the *synoptic* gospels because they can be "read together" (from the Greek word *syn*—"together" and *optic*—"look at"). Their many similarities make comparisons helpful.

Each of the evangelists tailored his sources to fit his particular outlook on Jesus and to address the religious needs of the Christians for whom he was writing. This is why sometimes you will find slight changes in the same material used by the synoptic gospel writers.

John's gospel, the most highly developed gospel, was the last composed. It doesn't seem to depend heavily on the other three.

Please study carefully the following chart to get a bird's-eye view of each gospel. Someone once summarized the gospels this way: "Matthew presents Jesus as the Royal Savior; Mark, as the Servant of humanity; Luke, as the Son of humanity; John, as the Son of God."

Gospel	Author	Date	Intended Audience	Major Theological Slant
Mark	John Mark, a close follower of Peter, perhaps his interpreter	shortly after the death of Peter (A.D. 64), as early as A.D. 65 or perhaps as late as A.D. 70	Christians (perhaps in Rome), who are trying to understand what it means to suffer for Christ	centers around the titles *Christ* and *Son of Man*; to follow Jesus means to suffer like he did
Matthew	author unknown, perhaps a former Jewish scribe; could be based on early version written in Aramaic	sometime after the destruction of the Jewish Temple in A.D. 70 (perhaps between A.D. 75-85)	a Jewish-Christian audience	Jesus is the Messiah-king prophesied in the Old Testament; he is a teacher who surpasses Moses

| Luke | Luke, a physician, the secretary of St. Paul and the author of the Acts of the Apostles | suggested dates range from A.D. 75-85 | a Gentile-Christian audience | Jesus came for everyone; Jesus cares for everyone, especially the poor, the outcast, etc. |
| John | written and edited by close disciples of St. John the Apostle, the "beloved disciple" | sometime between A.D. 90-100 | for the Christian churches around the Roman empire | Jesus is God's Word, superior to all prophets; Jesus is the norm for religious belief and practice. |

Mark's Jesus: The Servant Messiah

Mark, probably a secretary of the apostle Peter, wrote the earliest gospel around the year A.D. 65. It concentrates on the deeds of Jesus, rather than his words. It does seem to have some connection to the oral preaching of Peter. Compared to the other gospels, the portrait of Jesus in Mark's gospel is vivid, human and down to earth.

Mark wrote his gospel for a Gentile-Christian audience, perhaps in Rome, which was undergoing persecution. A major theme of the gospel is that to follow Jesus means that a Christian must suffer like Jesus did. Mark's gospel, then, presents a Suffering Messiah for Christians to imitate.

A Down-to-Earth Jesus.   There is no doubt that Mark proclaims Jesus' proper identity: "the gospel about Jesus Christ, the Son of God" (Mk 1:1). But Mark's gospel tells us that Jesus was human, too. For example, when Jesus met the skepticism of his critical countrymen before curing a man with a withered hand, Mark writes:

> Then he looked *angrily* round at them, grieved to find
> them so obstinate . . . (Mk 3:5, italics added).

Matthew and Luke do not mention that Jesus was angry. They toned down other details Mark included, especially if these details might cast Jesus in an unfavorable light. For example, Mark minces no words when he reports that Jesus' family said,

> "He is out of his mind" (Mk 3:21).

Matthew and Luke drop this quote from their report of what Jesus' kinsmen thought of him. Mark also pointedly reports that Jesus "could work no miracle" (6:5) in his home town of Nazareth because people lacked faith. Luke drops this story altogether, perhaps because he didn't want his readers to get the wrong idea about Jesus' power. Matthew, on the other hand, changes Mark's "could not" to

> "he did not work many miracles there because of their
> lack of faith" (Mt 13:58).

Mark's portrait of Jesus has a ring of authenticity to it. In it, Jesus curses a fig tree (Mk 11:12-14), a scene Luke changes to a parable. Jesus also warmly embraces children who approach him. And at the calming of the storm, Mark gives us a vivid detail not recorded by the other evangelists:

> He was in the stern, his head on a cushion, asleep (Mk
> 4:38).

Mark's Jesus is the Son of God, but he is also human like us, one who has real emotions like anger and compassion and real needs like sleep.

Jesus: Messiah and Son of Man.   Scholars consider Chapter 8:27-33 to be the key passage in Mark's gospel. You'll note two things: (1) Jesus accepts the title *Christ* which Peter gives to him. (2) Jesus immediately begins to use the title *Son of Man* to describe himself and then teaches that he will be a *Suffering Servant* for his people.

The English word *Christ* comes from the Greek word *Christos*, a translation for the Hebrew word *Messiah*, which means "anointed one." Many of Jesus' contemporaries had different ideas of what the Messiah would be. Mark tells us consistently that Jesus accepts this important title but that he was reluctant to let people know of his identity. No doubt he did this because his concept of the "anointed one" was radically different from that of his people and disciples.

After Jesus accepts Peter's proclamation of his true identity, he warns Peter not to tell anyone. Then Jesus tells the apostles that he is the Son of Man who will suffer and die for his people. *Son of Man* comes from a prophecy in Daniel where the glorious Messiah is called "Son of Man" (Dn 7:13). Many times throughout the gospels Jesus refers to himself with this title. However, he also understands this title in light of the prophecies of Isaiah who sees the Messiah as a Suffering Servant (Is 42-53). For Jesus, the Son of Man is both a Messiah who will come in glory (Daniel), but only after he has suffered and sacrificed his life for his people (Isaiah).

Peter has difficulty accepting Jesus' interpretation of the Messiah's true identity. He argues with Jesus. Jesus realizes that Peter is tempting him away from his true vocation and compares him to Satan, who judges not by God's standards but by human standards.

Mark's gospel tells us that Jesus is indeed the Messiah. But Jesus is not an earthly, kingly Messiah. His leadership is the way of the cross. Not until the resurrection, ascension and glorification of Jesus would the early Christian community begin to understand Jesus' way.

A key message of Mark's gospel is that to follow Jesus means to pick up our daily cross in imitation of him. Suffering for the Lord, though, leads to salvation and our participation in his glorious resurrection. In conclusion, the evangelist Mark proclaims that even *suffering* Christians can *celebrate* the good news of Jesus because Jesus brings eternal life.

Jesus the Messiah

In Jesus' day most Jews expected a messiah to come to save them. This belief came from Old Testament prophets who had varying images of the messiah.

Please read the following prophetic references to the messiah. Describe the kind of messiah prophesied.

Is 9:5-7	Is 53:6-7
Is 40:10-11	Mi 5:1-4
Is 52:13	Mal 3:1-5

Then read the following passages from Mark's gospel.

Mk 2:1-12   Mk 11:1-11

Discuss the actions and teachings of Jesus that made people think of him as the Messiah.

■ *discuss* ■

With your classmates, discuss what it might mean to suffer for Jesus today.

Matthew's Jesus: The New Moses

Church fathers from the earliest centuries tell us that the apostle Matthew composed an early version of a gospel in Aramaic, Jesus' own tongue, perhaps sometime in the early 40s. Our gospel of Matthew, written in Greek for Jewish-Christians, dates from around A.D. 75-85. It could be based on this earlier Aramaic gospel as well as Mark's gospel, Q, and other materials available only to the author of this gospel.

The author of the gospel was probably a Jewish scribe who had a thorough knowledge of Palestine and Jewish customs. In its liturgies and catechetical instructions, the early church used Matthew's gospel more frequently than the other three.

The author of Matthew divided his gospel into five books, plus the infancy and the passion narratives. This five-book arrangement, centered on five key sermons, suggests that the author of Matthew wished to present Jesus as the New Moses, the teacher of the New Law. The first five books of the Old Testament—the Pentateuch—contains the Torah or Law given to Moses to teach to the Chosen People. A narrative section precedes the five sermons. Here is an outline of the sermons:

Art by Robert Hodgell

Narrative	Sermons
Ch. 3-4: The beginning of Jesus' public life	*Ch. 5-7*: Sermon on the Mount (ethics of God's reign)
Ch. 8-9: Ten miracles to reveal who Jesus is	*Ch. 10*: Sermon to the apostles (their mission to spread the reign of God)
Ch. 11-12: Pharisees oppose Jesus	*Ch. 13*: Sermon of the parables (Jesus defends the reign of God)
Ch. 14-17: Jesus teaches the apostles	*Ch 18*: Sermon on church leadership
Ch. 19-23: Jesus meets further opposition	*Ch. 24-25*: Sermon on the coming of the reign of God

Please read Mt 18.

1. How do you achieve greatness in God's kingdom?

2. What will happen if we cause scandal to others?

3. What three steps must be taken if a Christian brother or sister needs correction?

a.

b.

c.

The very organization of Matthew's gospel suggests that he focused on Jesus the teacher. Jesus' words have prime importance. You can see this when you read the Sermon on the Mount in which Jesus is compared to Moses. Where Moses handed down the Ten Commandments, Jesus hands down the eight Beatitudes, the ethics of a new law. This remarkable sermon presents Jesus as an authoritative teacher. He clearly knows that God's reign is here, and he wants to communicate to his disciples what this means for daily living.

Even today we can learn much of what it means to follow Jesus by studying the five sermons in Matthew's gospel.

▪ *discuss* ▪

What is the meaning of the parable of the unforgiving debtor? How might this parable apply to us in our own daily lives?

A second emphasis in Matthew's gospel shows Jewish-Christian readers that Jesus is indeed the Messiah promised in the Hebrew scriptures. For example, Matthew uses the title "Son of David," a clear reference to the Messiah, more than any other evangelist. Matthew frequently uses Old

Testament prophecies to proclaim the true identity of Jesus. He wants his readers to realize that the Hebrew scriptures have reached their fulfillment in Jesus Christ.

Prophecies

Read any five of the following passages from Matthew's gospel and its corresponding Old Testament prophecy. In parallel columns in your notebook, note what each passage says.

Matthew		*Old Testament*
1:22-23	(Jesus born of a virgin)	Is 7:14
2:5-6	(Born in Bethlehem)	Mi 5:1
2:15	(Flight into Egypt)	Hos 11:1
2:18	(Slaughter of the Innocents)	Jer 31:15
4:15-16	(Ministry in Galilee)	Is 8:23—9:1
12:18-21	(Serving by leading)	Is 42:1-4
13:14-15	(Spiritual blindness)	Is 6:9-10
13:35	(Teaching in parables)	Ps 78:2
21:5	(Entry into Jerusalem on a donkey)	Is 62:11; Zec 9:9
27:9-10	(Judas betrays Jesus)	Zec 11:12-13

Luke's Jesus: Savior of the World

Tradition tells us that Luke, a Gentile convert to Christianity, was both a medical doctor and a companion to St. Paul. Luke wrote between A.D. 75-85 for a Gentile-Christian audience. Luke, a highly polished writer, chooses the city of Jerusalem as a key symbol throughout his gospel.

The Messianic age begins in Jerusalem, and the second part of Jesus' ministry centers on a journey to the Holy City. The drama of salvation unfolds there. From Jerusalem, the apostles will preach the message of Jesus Christ to the end of the world.

Additionally, Luke highlights two major themes throughout his literary masterpiece: (1) The gospel of Jesus is truly good news and a cause of celebration; (2) Jesus is a universal savior who brings salvation to Jew and Gentile alike.

Jesus' Message Is One of Joy.   Perhaps the heart of Luke's gospel is Chapter 15, which gives us the parables of the lost sheep, the lost coin and the Prodigal Son. These parables announce that God's forgiveness of sinners is a cause for celebration. Jesus proclaims time and again:

> "I tell you, there is rejoicing among the angels of God over one repentant sinner" (Lk 15:10).

Through his actions and his message, Jesus brought God to people. His gentleness, his compassion, his sensitivity are all signs of God's healing love.

> All the people were overjoyed at all the wonders he worked (Lk 13:17).

Jesus Is for Everyone.   Luke's Jesus sought out those people we would call "losers" — lepers, Samaritans, tax collectors and other sinners. Luke's gospel also underscores Jesus' revolutionary attitude toward women. They came to him for cures, anointed his feet and were his constant companions. Mary and Martha are his friends. His pity for the widow of Nain prompts him to raise her son from the dead. In Luke, Jesus' mother is singled out as the model believer. Only his gospel has Mary's beautiful Magnificat (1:46-55), a deep prayer of faith and submission to God's will.

Jesus' compassion is evident throughout Luke's gospel and symbolized best in Jesus' dying moments. While he was being crucified, taunted and tormented by his executioners, he says:

> "Father, forgive them; they do not know what they are doing" (Lk 23:34).

And with his last ounce of energy he thinks of the good thief hanging in misery next to him, promising him paradise.

Luke's Jesus is *everyone's* compassionate Savior. His love has no limits. Luke's message is clear: We should allow Jesus to live in us so we can love everyone—saint and sinner—in imitation of our Lord.

Compassionate Touch

Jesus showed his compassion through the healing power of touch. Luke often portrays Jesus showing love through the sense of touch. Read the following passages in Luke's gospel and note in your journal how Jesus touched people.

4:40-41	8:40-56
5:12-16	13:10-13
7:11-17	18:15-17

▪ *discuss* ▪

As a class, come up with a list of people who need the healing touch of compassion. (For example, lonely old folks who yearn for visitors.) Make a list of at least 10 categories of people. Then decide what you can do as an individual to show God's compassion to these individuals. Make a resolution to do so and then report back to your classmates what you *felt* in sharing love this way.

John's Jesus: The Word of God

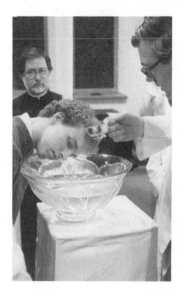

John's gospel is the most theologically developed of the four gospels. Finally edited by disciples of John the Apostle sometime between A.D. 90-100, it stresses more than the other gospels the *significance* of Jesus' life and words. In light of the resurrection and with the help of the Holy Spirit, the true meaning of Jesus can now be understood.

John's gospel contains many rich themes, for example, ones that relate to Christian worship and the theology of the sacraments (especially baptism and the Eucharist). But a major focus is on Jesus as *Word of God*. Note the opening lines of the gospel:

> In the beginning was the Word:
> the Word was with God
> and the Word was God.
>
> The Word was the real light
> that gives light to everyone;
> he was coming into the world.
>
> The Word became flesh,
> he lived among us,
> and we saw his glory,
> the glory that he has from the Father as only Son of
>   the Father,
> full of grace and truth   (Jn 1:1,9,14).

Underscored in John's gospel, then, is the mystery of the *Incarnation*, that is, God's Son becoming flesh in Jesus Christ. The title *Word of God* stresses that Jesus was a *mediator*, one who came with a message from the Father. Jesus himself — his word and his deeds — is the message; he is God the Father's perfect word, his perfect self-expression. As our words give a reality to our ideas, so is the Word of God (Jesus Christ) God-made-flesh. Jesus is God in a form that we can see, touch and listen to. He is the visible sign of the invisible God.

What is the major implication of looking at Jesus this way? By studying Jesus' words and actions and reflecting on his suffering and death, we can discover much about God—who he is and what he wants for us. Jesus came to show us the way, to shed light on our lives.

"I am the Way; I am Truth and Life.
No one can come to the Father except through me" (Jn 14:6).

John's gospel gives many images to teach how vitally important Jesus is for our salvation. Jesus is the bread of life, living water, the sheepgate, the good shepherd, the true vine, the light of the world, the resurrection and the life. His words contain eternal life. If we live them and unite ourselves to our Lord, he promises us the greatest gift of all—eternal life:

> "I am the resurrection.
> Anyone who believes in me, even though that
>   person dies, will live,
> and whoever lives and believes in me
> will never die.
> Do you believe this?" (Jn 11:25-26).

Faith in Jesus

Please read John 6 where Jesus stresses the theme of "bread of life." In this beautiful homily, Jesus asks his disciples for faith in him. He should outrank everything else. His words bring life. Examine your level of commitment to Jesus at this stage of your faith journey. Rank yourself on the following items according to this scale:

1 — this describes me well
2 — I need some improvement
3 — I need much improvement

_____ **Faith in Jesus:** Jesus said, "Whoever sees me, sees the one who sent me" (Jn 12:45). I know that Jesus is the #1 priority in my life.

_____ **Things:** I realize that my personal possessions are gifts from God, but I realize that they will never be the source of true happiness.

_____ **Eucharist:** Jesus is the "bread of life." I receive him worthily at least once a week at Sunday Mass.

_____ **Scripture:** To hear Jesus is to hear God. I listen to his word by reading the Bible on a regular basis.

_____ **Gratitude:** Jesus thanked God for answering his prayer when he raised Lazarus from the dead (Jn 11:41-42). I thank Jesus for the life he has given me, for my family, friends, my health, education and other gifts.

_____ **Prayer:** Jesus said: "Whatever you ask for in my name I will do, so that the Father may be glorified in the Son" (Jn 14:13). I pray often in Jesus' name.

_____ **Obedience:** Jesus said: "If you love me you will keep my commandments" (Jn 14:15). I abide by Jesus' command.

_____ **Other People:** Jesus came so we might have life. I try to be a source of life for others, for example, by being sensitive to their needs.

▪ *summary* ▪

1. Jesus is the good news, the gospel, he came to preach. *Matthew, Mark, Luke* and *John* are the four written versions of the gospel.

2. The gospels resulted from three stages of development: (a) the historical life of Jesus; (b) the oral preaching of the early church; (c) the written gospels themselves.

There was much else that Jesus did; if it were written down in detail, I do not suppose the world itself would hold all the books that would be written.
—John 21:25

3. The gospels are authentic, inspired, written, communal expressions of the good news of Jesus Christ.

4. The gospels of Matthew, Mark and Luke are known as the *synoptic gospels.* They can be read together because of their many similarities. Matthew and Luke drew on an early version of Mark and also shared another common source designated as *Q*.

5. Mark's gospel stresses Jesus as the anointed one of God, the Messiah (or Christ). But Jesus interprets Christ to be a Suffering Servant, one who will die for his people before he comes in glory. The title *Son of Man* underscores Jesus' identification as a humble man, but also refers to his triumph at the end of time (cf. Dn 7:13).

6. Matthew casts Jesus as the New Moses, one who comes as a teacher of the law of love. He is also the "Son of David," the one promised in the Hebrew Scriptures who would come to deliver the people.

7. Luke's Jesus is the universal Savior, one who has come to liberate Jew and Gentile alike. Jesus especially seeks out the "losers" to show that the good news applies to everyone. Because this is so, joyful response to the gospel of Jesus predominates throughout Luke's masterpiece.

8. John's gospel reveals that Jesus is the Word of God who has come to reveal the Father's will. Jesus shows us the way to salvation. He is the mediator, the go-between, for God and us.

▪ *focus questions* ▪

1. Why is ignorance of scripture ignorance of Christ?

2. How did the gospels come to be? Give the dates for each of the stages in their formation.

3. When did Jesus die?

4. Explain reasons why the gospels eventually had to be written down.

5. Briefly explain the following elements for each of the four gospels:

   a. Date of composition
   b. Author
   c. Audience
   d. Major theological theme
   e. What the gospel says about Jesus

6. Explain the meaning of these titles of Jesus:

Christ	Son of David
Son of Man	Universal Savior
New Moses	Son of God
Suffering Servant	Word of God

7. Identify and define the following key terms:

gospel	Incarnation
kerygma	synoptic gospels

journal entries

1. This chapter discussed several titles of Jesus found in the gospels. Some of these you can find in question 6 above. Others include the following: bread of life, living water, the sheepgate, the good shepherd, the true vine, the light of the world, the resurrection, the way, truth and life. Select one of these and write a short essay on what it means to you to call Jesus by this title.

2. *Enriching your vocabulary.*   Using a good dictionary, look up the meaning of the following terms. Write them in your journal.

anonymous	scandal
mince	skepticism
obstinate	stature

Prayer Reflection

Jesus gave us a new way to live when he gave us the eight Beatitudes. Pray them here and then reflect on their meaning in your life.

How blessed are the poor in spirit:
the kingdom of Heaven is theirs.
Blessed are *the gentle:*
they shall have the earth as inheritance.
Blessed are those who mourn:
they shall be comforted.
Blessed are those who hunger and thirst for
uprightness:
they shall have their fill.
Blessed are the merciful:
they shall have mercy shown them.
Blessed are the pure in heart:
they shall see God.
Blessed are the peacemakers:
they shall be recognized as children of God.
Blessed are those who are persecuted in the cause of
uprightness:
the kingdom of Heaven is theirs.

—Matthew 5:3-10

▪ *reflection* ▪

Examine how well you are living the Beatitudes. Use the following scale:

    4 — this describes me very well
    3 — this describes me most of the time
    2 — this describes me some of the time
    1 — I need work on this

_____ poor in spirit

_____ gentle

_____ concerned about justice

_____ merciful

_____ pure in heart

_____ peacemaker

▪ *resolution* ▪

Memorize the Beatitudes. Take one and try to do something to make it happen in your life this coming week.

chapter 7
Jesus
A Personal Portrait

He is a path, if any be misled;
   He is a robe, if any naked be;
If any chance to hunger, he is bread;
   If any be a bondman, he is free;
   If any be but weak, how strong is he!
To dead men life is he, to sick men health;
To blind men sight, and to the needy wealth;
A pleasure without loss, a
   treasure without stealth.

—Giles Fletcher (1588-1623)

In This Chapter

We will look at:

- the human Jesus
- Jesus as friend
- the strong, gentle Jesus
- the honest, courageous Jesus
- Jesus and women

A rabbi once asked his students, "When do we know that night has ended and the day begun?"

One student offered this answer: "Is it when you can tell the difference between a sheep and a dog?"

"No," replied the rabbi.

"Is it," asked another, "when you can detect the difference between an olive tree and a fig tree?"

"Wrong again," said the rabbi.

"Then when is it?" asked the students. And the rabbi answered:

"It is the moment when you can look at a face you have never seen before and recognize this person as your brother or sister. Until then, no matter how bright the day, it is still the night."

The lesson of the rabbi is the essential message taught by Jesus. Everyone is our brother or sister; we have a common loving Abba.

Jesus is our Redeemer and our teacher. Jesus is also our brother. He looks at our faces and sees reflected in them the image of his Father.

Jesus invites us to take a careful look at him, too. "Who do you say that I am?" What do you see when you look at Jesus? When you study his life, what admirable qualities do you see in him?

131

The Human Jesus

The New Testament's portrait of Jesus clearly tells us that he is human like us. He shared our life—joys and sorrows, good times and bad. Because he knows us, he can teach us how to live.

What do you know about the *human* side of Jesus? Test your knowledge by answering the following questions *true* or *false*.

____ 1. Jesus received instant knowledge about everything; he did not have to learn.

____ 2. Jesus had special friends.

____ 3. Jesus never got angry.

____ 4. Jesus never wanted to start a church.

____ 5. Jesus said it was OK to pay taxes.

____ 6. Jesus knew the exact hour of the world's end.

____ 7. Jesus was never bothered by hunger or thirst.

____ 8. Jesus was tempted to sin, and he did sin.

____ 9. Women were among the disciples of Jesus.

____ 10. Jesus drank wine and enjoyed good meals.

▪ *journal* ▪

Check your answers by reading the following New Testament passages. Note in your journal what each passage says about Jesus.

1. Lk 1:32	6. Mk 13:32
2. Jn 21:20; 11:3,35-36	7. Jn 4:6
3. Mk 11:15-19	8. Jn 4:14-15
4. Mt 16:18	9. Lk 8:1-3
5. Lk 20:20-26	10. Lk 7:31-35

Although the gospels do not show us the physical face of Jesus, they do paint a picture of the *kind of person* he must have been. Let us now sketch some key features revealed about Jesus in the gospels.

Jesus as Friend

"You can tell a person by his or her friends." Apply this cliché to Jesus and you can tell a lot about him. Look at the apostles, for example. Peter was a headstrong, impetuous man. Or look at Zebedee's sons—the brothers John and James. So fiery were their tempers that Jesus nicknamed them "sons of thunder." A hated tax collector befriended Jesus; ordinary fishermen left their boats and traipsed after him; the maimed and sick longed to touch him and be by his side. Jesus had influential friends, men like Joseph of Arimathea who was a member of the Sanhedrin. But he also had friends with whom "decent people" did not associate. For example, the Pharisees criticized Jesus' friendship with tax-gatherers and sinners.

People saw in Jesus an extraordinary human being. They craved his friendship. Friendship-love (*philia* in the Greek) is essential for full, productive living. Without it we wither and die psychologically. Many of Jesus' contemporaries wanted to be Jesus' friends because they sensed in him the source of true life.

Jesus needed friends, too. He was especially close to the youngest apostle, John, and to Lazarus and his sisters Mary and Martha. Jesus so loved John that, as he hung dying on the cross, he entrusted his own mother to John's care (see Jn 19:26-27). John was like a brother to Jesus. And when he heard of Lazarus' death, Jesus wept. Jesus loved his friends deeply. His loyalty and devotion to them and his willingness to die for them exemplify the very meaning of friendship.

Jesus calls *you* his friend, too. Reflect on what he has to say:

> "You are my friends,
> if you do what I command you. . . .
> I call you friends. . . .
> You did not choose me,
> no, I chose you. . . .
> My command to you
> is to love one another"   (Jn 15:14-17).

Jesus loves you unconditionally. You are special to him. He sees in you something so worthwhile that he chooses

you to do his work. He gives you many gifts: your parents, your friends, your intellect, your talents, your health, food, shelter.

Jesus will never take away his invitation to friendship. We may sin and deny his love, we may misuse our gifts, we may hurt others and turn from God—but Jesus always invites us to accept his friendship. Nothing in this life, no one's opinion of us, can possibly compare to Jesus' earth-shaking proclamation, "I call you friend."

Friendship

The following traits typify good friendships. Rate yourself according to your relationship with your best friend and with Jesus.

> 4 — describes me very well
> 3 — describes me most of the time
> 2 — describes me some of the time
> 1 — I need lots of improvement here

	Friend	*Jesus*
a. I spend time with my friend/ Jesus.	_____	_____
b. I listen to my friend/Jesus.	_____	_____
c. I accept my friend/Jesus.	_____	_____
d. I admire my friend/Jesus.	_____	_____
e. I love my friend/Jesus.	_____	_____
f. I give to my friend/Jesus.	_____	_____
g. I graciously receive from my friend/Jesus.	_____	_____
h. I am totally honest with my friend/Jesus.	_____	_____
i. I am not afraid to tell others about my friendship.	_____	_____

▪ *discuss* ▪

With your classmates, please discuss how you can exhibit each of the qualities listed above in your relationship with the Lord.

The Strong, Gentle Jesus

The following passage tells us a lot about Jesus' character:

> People were bringing little children to him, for him to touch them. The disciples scolded them, but when Jesus saw this he was indignant and said to them, "Let the little children come to me; do not stop them; for it is to such as these that the kingdom of God belongs. In truth I tell you, anyone who does not welcome the kingdom of God like a little child will never enter it." Then he embraced them, laid his hands on them and gave them his blessing (Mk 10:13-16).

This passage reveals both the strength and gentleness of Jesus. *Indignant* also means angry, incensed or irate. These are strong words. Jesus was upset that his disciples would deny children access to him. And he let them know his opinion.

This is not the only time that we meet a forceful Jesus in the New Testament. You may remember the scene of Jesus clearing the Temple of money changers. Jesus drove home the message that his Father's house was a place of prayer, not a place for crass business transactions.

Jesus could not tolerate hypocrisy. Jesus accuses some of the scribes and Pharisees of laying heavy burdens on the consciences of the simple people while they themselves did not do what they taught. He also said they showed off in their religious practices so people would think well of them.

Jesus used some strong words with these false teachers. He repeatedly called them *hypocrites.* To this charge he added *blind guides, fools, serpents,* and *brood of vipers*! It takes courage to vent this kind of anger on men who had the power in society and the religious establishment. But Jesus was trying to shock them into changing their ways and seeking repentance. Jesus paid a price for his convictions. His enemies plotted against him and ultimately killed him.

Jesus was a man of passionate convictions, but these did not get in the way of his tender, loving, sensitive presence to others. Picture the little children coming to Jesus and his warm acceptance of them. Jesus tenderly embraced them and made them feel wanted and loved.

Jesus' touch reached out to comfort Peter, James and John, frightened by the vision of God's glory shining through Jesus at the Transfiguration. Jesus knew how frightened his apostles were, and he sought to reassure them by his gentle touch. He also touched repulsive lepers and cured them. He laid his hands on many other sick people as well. Jesus felt for the hurting and responded to their needs.

Jesus could sense when people needed him. Luke gives a dramatic example of this. One day Jesus was in a large crowd of people, all of whom were pressing in on him. A certain woman who had been bleeding for 12 years came up behind him and brushed the tassel of his cloak. She was immediately cured. Jesus asked, "Who was it that touched me?" Peter suggested that it was the crowds, but Jesus said that someone definitely touched him.

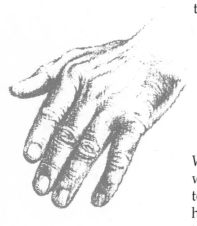

> Seeing herself discovered, the woman came forward trembling, and falling at his feet explained in front of all the people why she had touched him and how she had been cured at that very moment. "My daughter," he said, "your faith has saved you; go in peace" (Lk 8:47-48).

Jesus' gentleness translated into compassion for sinners. When Simon the Pharisee invited Jesus to dinner, a sinful woman rushed in off the streets to anoint his feet with her tears. Simon thought ugly thoughts about her, condemning her and also condemning Jesus for allowing himself to be touched by her. But Jesus forgave her sins and told her to leave joyfully and sin no more.

A true portrait of Jesus must capture both his compassion for others and his strength in confronting evil.

Jesus: Strong, Yet Gentle

1. Please read the following gospel passages. They help sketch Jesus' character. Then write a few paragraphs in

your journal describing what you think Jesus was like as a person. Share your essay in class.

Mk 1:40-45	Lk 7:36-50
Mk 14:43-65	Lk 23:29-43
Mt 15:32-39	Jn 8:1-11
Mt 23:1-36	Jn 13:1-5

2. Be aware of people you meet during the day. Identify a person who needs your compassion, your friendship, your gentleness. Perhaps a brother, sister or parent has had a tough day. Perhaps a lonely classmate never seems to have any friends. Maybe an old person on a bus needs a seat or someone to talk to.

Then do something for this person. A kind word or an interest in what the person is saying could be concrete ways to serve those who need your love.

Write in your journal what you learned about other people and yourself by observing them and responding in a special way to their hurt and loneliness.

The Honest, Courageous Jesus

Jesus taught humility and honesty and modeled both of these virtues himself. He told his disciples not to parade their good deeds in public just to attract notice and instructed them to give alms discreetly without drawing attention to their charity. He backed up his words about humility with *actions* that show us the very meaning of humility. At the Last Supper, Jesus washed the feet of his apostles, a menial task that even slaves were not required to do. Jesus explained his actions in this way:

> "Do you understand," he said, "what I have done to you? You call me Master and Lord, and rightly; so I am. If I, then, the Lord and Master, have washed your feet, you must wash each other's feet. I have given you an example so that you may copy what I have done to you" (Jn 13:12-15).

Jesus never asks us to do what he has not already done. He lived what he preached. In his teaching on love, Jesus says true love even extends to our enemies. We should do good even to those who hate us. We can only do this if we forgive. Forgiveness and love of enemies go hand in hand. Jesus himself forgave everyone who asked, even his executioners:

> "Father, forgive them; they do not know what they are doing" (Lk 23:34).

Jesus' passion and death are the greatest testimony to his genuine honesty and love. He taught:

> "No one can have greater love
> than to lay down his life for his friends" (Jn 15:13)

and then surrendered his own life for us, showing his honesty, his authenticity and mostly his love.

▪ *journal* ▪

Do you back up your words with action? Give examples.

Are you a person of your word? Can people count on you? Give examples.

Who is the most genuine person you know?

What makes this person so special in your eyes?

What do you find most admirable about Jesus Christ? Why?

Discuss your responses with your classmates.

Jesus and Women

Jesus was a man of his people; but in some ways he was unique. We can see this in the way he treated women. Jews in the first century considered women to be inferior to men. Women were not allowed to study the Torah (Law) and only rarely were they taught to read or write. They were not required to recite morning prayers, prayers at meals and other Jewish prayers. They had no official part in the synagogue and were only permitted to sit behind a screen or on a balcony.

Men were not even supposed to speak with their wives, daughters or sisters in public. Only rarely were women allowed to testify in court and they could not divorce their husbands, though at the time it was easy and common for men to divorce their wives for almost any reason.

Every male recited this prayer daily:

> Praised be God that he has not created me a gentile;
> praised be God that he has not created me a woman;
> praised be God that he has not created me an
>   ignorant man.

Jesus showed in many ways that women were also God's children, equal to men. Luke specifically tells us that women followed Jesus around as his disciples and that he taught them, even though the custom of his day was not to associate with women in public.

Women were also instrumental in the three resurrection miracles Jesus performed during his public ministry. First, he raised the daughter of Jairus. Second, he took compassion on the widow of Nain by raising her son. Third, he raised his friend Lazarus from the dead at the tearful request of his sisters Mary and Martha. Moreover, the gospels tell us that Jesus appeared first to Mary Magdalene, a fact that the eleven apostles refused to believe because, like most men of their day, they mistrusted women.

Jesus conversed with a Samaritan woman at a well. Even the apostles were surprised by this behavior: She was not only a woman, but a hated Samaritan as well. He even told this woman that he was the very Messiah she was awaiting. On another occasion, Jesus' enemies wanted to trap Jesus into condemning a woman caught in adultery. But Jesus forgave her and told her to sin no more. On still another occasion, his enemies criticized him for allowing a sinful woman to anoint his feet. Jesus refused to judge her negatively; rather, he forgave her sins and told her to go in peace.

Jesus' actions proved that he held women in high regard. His teachings showed the same attitude. For example, when his enemies wanted him to take sides on what conditions a man may divorce his wife, Jesus simply forbade divorce altogether. He said that God wanted married people to stay together for life. He also refused to treat women as sex objects. They were persons who should be treated with respect:

"If a man looks at a woman lustfully, he has already committed adultery with her in his heart" (Mt 5:28).

Jesus' high regard for women also shows up in his teaching. For example, Jesus often used women in his stories and sayings, something the rabbis of his day rarely did. His images of women were always positive, in marked contrast to his contemporaries.

Jesus' attitude toward women gives us a wonderful insight into his character. He challenged people of his day—and our own day—to treat women as equal to men in dignity, worthy of the utmost respect. They are precious sisters in a human family that reflects God's beauty and wisdom. In God's kingdom there are no second-class citizens. The way he treated others with love, gentleness, strength, sensitivity, honesty and humility shows us how best to live as *his* brothers and sisters.

▪ *summary* ▪

1. Jesus reveals himself as a *friend.* Jesus had many special friends like Lazarus, Martha and Mary, and John the Apostle. The essence of the gospel is that Jesus also calls us his friends.

2. Jesus was strong in his challenge to the scribes to live what they preached. Yet, he was *gentle,* for example, when he welcomed children in God's name.

3. Jesus was *honest* and *courageous.* He lived his message of love, especially when he freely surrendered his life on a cross so we might have eternal life.

4. Jesus' character is starkly revealed in the way he treated women. His actions and words tell us that women are equal to men and worthy of the utmost respect.

▪ *focus questions* ▪

1. List and discuss three character traits revealed about Jesus in the gospels. Give scriptural evidence to illustrate your choices.

2. "I call *you,* friend." What might Jesus mean by this?

3. How did Jesus treat women? What does this reveal about his character?

4. Select three passages from the gospels that you think capture the essential character of Jesus. Explain what they reveal about him.

▪ *journal entries* ▪

1. Write an essay that discusses:
   a. how *you* are most like Jesus
   b. why Jesus would want to be your friend

2. *Enriching your vocabulary.* Using a good dictionary, look up the meaning of the following terms. Write the definitions in your journal.

charisma	impetuous
compatible	menial
discreet	stealth

Prayer Reflection

Icons are religious images painted by artists who seek to be God's channel, allowing God's spirit to guide the brush. Icons are often described as "windows to heaven," where God can touch us here on earth.

Icon in Greek means image. When we pray before icons we put ourselves in the presence of the holy person or enter into the religious mystery that is portrayed.

Here is a famous icon of Christ, the Creator of the Universe. Look at it as you recite over and over the Jesus Prayer, a prayer that stresses Jesus' identity and what he does for us. He is truly God's Son, the Messiah and our Savior.

GIRAUDON/ART RESOURCE

Lord, Jesus Christ,
Son of the Living God,
have mercy on me, a sinner.

▪ *reflection* ▪

What do you see in the eyes of Christ?

▪ *resolution* ▪

Recite the Jesus prayer at least 10 times a day for the next week or so.

chapter 8

The Paschal Mystery of Jesus

Passion, Death and Resurrection

Christ to protect me to-day
  against poison, against burning,
  against drowning, against wounding,
  so that there may come abundance of reward.
Christ with me, Christ before me, Christ behind me,
Christ in me, Christ beneath me, Christ above me,
Christ on my right, Christ on my left,
Christ where I lie, Christ where I sit,
  Christ where I arise,
Christ in the heart of everyone who thinks of me,
Christ in the mouth of everyone who speaks to me,
Christ in every eye that sees me,
Christ in every ear that hears me.

—St. Patrick (389-461)

In This Chapter

We will look at the following topics:

- the passion narratives
- events of the last week (Palm Sunday, Holy Thursday, Garden and Arrest)
- Jesus' trial before the Jewish authorities
- Jesus and Pilate
- the crucifixion
- the resurrection of Jesus
- the paschal mystery in our lives

A father used to say to his little boy, "How much do I love you?"

The little boy, who did not know the difference between the words *so* and *too*, answered, "You love me too much."

Of course, the father loved his little image and likeness so much, because parents can never love a child too much.

We might ask the same question about Jesus: How much does he love us? Look at Jesus on the cross with his arms outstretched. His open arms tells us that he loves us so much.

The cross is the symbol of our faith in Jesus. A sign of defeat and death has become a powerful symbol of God's love for us. Jesus' sacrifice on the cross has reconciled us to God. Jesus' *passion, death, resurrection* and *glorification* is the great *paschal mystery* of God's love. Through these important events of our faith we will reflect on the meaning of Jesus' love for us.

145

A Quiz

Before reading the passion narratives in Mark's and Matthew's gospels, check your knowledge of Jesus' final days. Mark the following + if the statement is true, 0 if the statement is false. Correct your own work by checking the passage given.

_____ 1. Pilate's wife wanted Jesus condemned to death. (Mt 27:19)

_____ 2. The chief priests approached Judas to try to bribe him to hand Jesus over to them. (Mk 14:10-11)

_____ 3. Jesus did not want to die. (Mk 14:35-37)

_____ 4. The crucifixion took place at Golgotha (an Aramaic word that means "the place of the skull"). (Mt 27:32-36)

_____ 5. Peter and James and John (the sons of Zebedee) witnessed Jesus' prayer in the Garden of Gethsemane. (Mt 26:36-37)

_____ 6. At the Last Supper, Jesus blessed the cup of wine _before_ blessing the bread. (Mk 14:22-25)

_____ 7. Jesus drank the wine mixed with myrrh that was offered to him on the cross. (Mk 15:23-26)

_____ 8. Jesus died at the sixth hour. (Mt 27:45)

_____ 9. The centurion who crucified Jesus acknowledged that he was the Son of God. (Mk 15:39)

_____ 10. Simon of Cyrene buried Jesus. (Mt 27:57-61)

▪ *journal* ▪

Prayerfully read the accounts of Jesus' passion and death in the gospels of Mark (chapters 14-15) and Matthew (chapters 26-27).

In your journal, please note 15 things you never thought before about Jesus' last hours.

Then, write a 300-word news article reporting what took place at the crucifixion. Assume the role of one of the characters who witnessed the crucifixion (examples: a soldier, an apostle, Mary, a passerby, one of Jesus' enemies). Share these in class.

The Passion Narratives

Palm Sunday.   Luke's gospel especially underscores the importance of Jerusalem in Jesus' ministry. At the Temple in Jerusalem people offered sacrifice and praise to thank God for God's many gifts. The important religious feasts like Passover and Pentecost drew pilgrims to the Temple from all around the Mediterranean world. Jesus himself approached Jerusalem on his last Passover with tears in his eyes. He knew its history well: It often scorned its prophets and put them to death.

However, the events of Jesus' last week before his death began on a high note. Jesus entered the city on the back of a colt to the triumphant cries of his disciples and followers. Here was God's Messiah:

> Blessed is he who is coming
> as King *in the name of the Lord!*
> Peace in heaven
> and glory in the highest heavens! (Lk 19:38).

Read Luke 19:28-48
Jesus enters Jerusalem in triumph

During the early days of Holy Week, Jesus spent his time teaching in the Temple precincts. He angered some of the Pharisees, chief priests and scribes because he criticized their hypocrisy. He also drove out the moneylenders from the Temple area.

> "*My house shall be a house of prayer* but you have turned it into *a bandits' den*"   (Lk 19:46).

Jesus' opponents tried to do away with him, but they could not find a chance because of Jesus' popularity with the people. Finally, a golden opportunity presented itself. Judas Iscariot, one of Jesus' apostles, agreed to turn Jesus over to them for 30 pieces of silver. He negotiated to do it at a time when the people would not know about it. Judas' chance came after the Passover meal Jesus celebrated with his apostles.

Read Luke 22 and John 13
the Last Supper

Holy Thursday — The Last Supper   Jesus longed to eat the Passover meal with his friends. For God's Chosen People, the Passover meal commemorated the miracle of God's love, recalling Yahweh's deliverance of the Hebrews from slavery in Egypt and their entry into the Holy Land after the 40-year Exodus experience.

At the Last Supper, Jesus celebrated a new Passover — the freedom from sin and death accomplished by his own death and resurrection. At this meal Jesus washed the feet of his disciples, a task even slaves did not have to perform. By doing so, Jesus taught them that the way of love is the way of service. To follow Jesus means to wash feet in imitation of him.

At this Passover meal Jesus gave himself to his friends in the form of bread and wine. Catholics believe our Lord instituted the sacrament of the Eucharist at the Last Supper. The Eucharist is a special sign of his love.

Today we celebrate the Eucharist in memory of Jesus who commanded us to "do this in remembrance of me" (Lk 22:19). It represents Jesus' free and total gift of his life poured out for us. It reenacts without blood and suffering his sacrifice on the cross. At this meal Jesus makes it very clear what he expects of all his followers:

> "I give you a new commandment:
> love one another;
> you must love one another
> just as I have loved you.
> It is by your love for one another,
> that everyone will recognize you
> as my disciples"   (Jn 13:34-35).

Read John 18:1-11
the agony in the garden and the arrest

The Garden and the Arrest.   After the Passover meal, Jesus retired with his apostles to the Garden of Gethsemane to pray. He withdrew from the others and knelt down. He knew that his testimony to the truth, his challenge to the religious leaders, would inevitably lead them to try to kill him. The thought of suffering and death frightened him as it would any normal human being. Jesus' severe mental anguish caused his sweat to fall to the ground like great drops of blood. Jesus prayed,

"Father, . . . if you are willing, take this cup away from me. Nevertheless, let your will be done, not mine" (Lk 22:42).

The disciples had fallen asleep. Jesus was alone in his agony. He remained faithful to his Father, however, not shirking his duty to witness to God's kingdom. He did not flee in spite of his fear.

Judas' betrayal came at night, when Jesus was away from his many supporters. Judas' kiss pointed out Jesus to the Temple guards and Jewish authorities. Some of the disciples reacted violently to the arrest. For example, Peter used his sword to cut off the right ear of Malchus, the high priest's servant. But the Man of Peace ordered his apostles to use no violence, and he healed the servant. Jesus allowed himself to be led away.

The Trial Before the Jewish Leaders. John's account of Jesus' trial before the Jewish leaders differs a bit from those of the synoptic gospels. Was there simply *one* trial at the high priest's house with the quickly assembled Jewish leaders? Or was there a preliminary hearing before Annas, the father-in-law of the high priest Caiaphas and then a later trial at Caiaphas' house? There is also some confusion about the exact day of Jesus' crucifixion. John states that it took place on the 14th day of Nisan, Passover Preparation Day. The synoptics, on the other hand, hold that it took place on the 15th day of Nisan, the day of the Passover itself.

We can probably never recover the exact chronology of Jesus' trial because the evangelists were writing a generation or more after the actual events. However, we can well imagine the charges against Jesus, and we can guess why his opponents wanted him to die.

Jesus was a threat to the Pharisees and the scribes. They appealed to tradition and the Law to figure out God's will. Jesus, on the other hand, claimed to know God's will intimately. He taught that God's salvation was taking place in his words and actions. He spoke and acted as though he stood in God's place. To a pious scribe or Pharisee, Jesus was misleading the people. To them, Jesus committed *blasphemy*, a grave sin where one claims divine powers and

Read John 18:12-27
trial before the Jewish leaders

privileges. Under Jewish law, this sin is punishable by death.

Jesus also upset the Sadducees, the aristocratic class that cooperated with Roman rule. They saw Jesus as a threat to the civil order and a danger to their position of leadership over the people. His prophetic act of cleansing the Temple made them nervous.

> "If we let him go on in this way everybody will believe in him, and the Romans will come and suppress the Holy Place and our nation" (Jn 11:48).

Caiaphas, the high priest, had the solution: Sacrifice Jesus and the whole nation will be preserved.

The Jewish trial had to show that Jesus was guilty of a crime punishable by death. Jewish law required witnesses to come forward to testify against Jesus. Unfortunately, the Jewish leaders could not produce any witnesses who agreed on what Jesus said, especially about destroying the Temple and rebuilding it in three days (see Jn 2:19). The witnesses contradicted themselves. If there were to be true justice, Jesus' trial should have concluded once the witnesses could not agree.

Caiaphas' last chance of convicting Jesus was to ask him directly:

> "Are you the Christ, the Son of the Blessed One?" "I am," said Jesus, "and you will see the *Son of man seated at the right hand of the Power and coming with the clouds of heaven*" (Mk 14:61-62).

Without any hesitation Jesus claimed that he is God's chosen one. Jesus' own words provided the Sanhedrin with the evidence needed to convict him of blasphemy. Caiaphas tore his robes and pronounced the death sentence against Jesus. Immediately some of the council members spat on Jesus, blindfolded him, hit his face and asked him to prophesy who it was that struck him. Jesus' torture was about to begin.

Read Luke 23:26-56
the crucifixion

The Trial Before Pilate. Roman occupation law did not allow the Jewish leaders to carry out the death penalty. Furthermore, Roman authorities did not consider the Jewish sin of *blasphemy*—insulting God's goodness by claiming equality with God or openly mocking God—a capital crime. In the Roman view, Jesus was simply a misguided prophet, strictly the concern of the Jews themselves.

The Jewish council realized that *leading the people astray* and *blasphemy* were two charges that Pilate, the Roman procurator, would simply toss out of court. They had to portray Jesus as a criminal in a way that would merit capital punishment—crucifixion—under Roman law. They did so by pressing the following charge:

> "We found this man inciting our people to revolt, opposing payment of the tribute to Caesar, and claiming to be Christ, a king" (Lk 23:2).

Jesus was far from a revolutionary. His whole ministry witnessed to peace, and he strongly denounced violence.

Pilate saw through the trumped-up charges brought against Jesus. Jesus simply did not look like a threat to Roman power. Pilate sensed that the Jewish leaders wanted to use him to further their ends, but he was not going to be duped so easily. So when he heard that Jesus was from Galilee, he saw a way out. His ploy was to send Jesus to Herod Antipas, in Jerusalem for the Passover, and ask him to decide Jesus' guilt or innocence.

Herod—called a fox by Jesus—had posted spies who kept tabs on Jesus, the wonder-worker. Herod finally found his opportunity to meet Jesus. He mockingly questioned Jesus and challenged him to perform a miracle. Jesus stood his ground and remained silent. At this, Herod was outraged. He and his followers contemptuously mocked and insulted Jesus. They draped a rich-looking robe on him and sent him back to Pilate. Herod's message was clear: Jesus is a harmless clown, a puppet-king. He is no threat to either Rome or to Pilate.

Pilate was now trapped; he had to decide. He knew that Jesus was innocent, so he tried to release him. He used the custom of freeing a prisoner during the Passover festivities. He believed the crowd would call for Jesus, an innocent man, over Barabbas, a known revolutionary who may have participated in a murder. However, Pilate's plan backfired.

The supporters of Barabbas and the handpicked backers of the Jewish leaders cried out for a guilty man over the innocent preacher from Nazareth.

What was Pilate to do? His plan to manipulate the crowd backfired. They screamed, "Crucify him!" And they shouted a threat he clearly understood:

> "If you set him free you are no friend of Caesar's; anyone who makes himself king is defying Caesar" (Jn 19:12).

This threat hit the politically sensitive Pilate where it hurt. No public official would be safe from the emperor's wrath if he permitted a false king to challenge Roman authority. Pilate knew the right thing to do: Free Jesus. However, he lacked moral courage. He did the *easy thing* to save his job: He ordered the crucifixion of Jesus.

Pilate felt tricked. But he had the last word. It was the custom to post the crime of crucified men above their crosses so pilgrims entering the city could see why a person was being tortured and killed. This sort of advertising had a chilling effect. To mock the Jewish authorities, Pilate posted this notice on Jesus' cross:

Jesus the Nazarene, King of the Jews.

The Jewish leaders were angry and wanted the sign changed to "He *claimed* to be the king of the Jews." However, Pilate was adamant.

The supreme irony is that Jesus is indeed the king of the Jews and of all people. His throne is the cross, the way of suffering and death.

Courage

The story of Jesus' passion reveals someone of immense courage and strength. It inspires us to imitate Jesus, to resist giving in to the easy way out.

How much fortitude do you have? How do you suffer for the Lord, for doing the right thing? Respond as honestly as you can to the following:

_____ 1. Everyone is cheating on a test. I would: a.) not cheat; b.) cheat; c.) I'm not sure what I'd do.

_____ 2. My friends are insulting a classmate whom they consider "a loser." I would: a.) join in the fun; b.) stand idly by; c.) try to get them to stop; d.) I'm not sure what I'd do.

_____ 3. At a party someone is using foul language, some of it directed toward Catholics and Jesus. I would: a.) be too afraid to say anything; b.) try to direct the conversation another way; c.) nicely correct the person; d.) I'm not sure what I'd do.

_____ 4. I come in long past my parents' curfew. When questioned where I was, I would: a.) be totally honest; b.) make up an excuse; c.) tell the truth if I had a good excuse, but make up a story if I did not; d.) I'm not sure what I would do.

▪ *discuss* ▪

1. What kind of action takes the most courage for a person your age? Explain.
2. In each of the examples above, how might a person *suffer* for doing the right thing?
3. Who is the most courageous person you know?

▪ *journal* ▪

Out of fear, Peter three times denied knowing Jesus. Picture Jesus looking at Peter from across the courtyard. (See Lk 22:54-62.) Write a short paragraph describing this scene. Tell your story from Peter's point of view.

Then, write Jesus a short letter telling him about a time you denied him. Let him look into *your* eyes. Write about what you see in Jesus' glance.

The Crucifixion. Someone once remarked that the way we die punctuates the sentence of our lives. It sums up what we stood for in life. If this observation is true, then Jesus' death proclaims what he lived: a life of love and forgiveness for everyone.

Pilate condemned Jesus to crucifixion, a horrible form of the death penalty widely used in the early centuries of the

Read Lk 23:26-56.

Roman Empire. It was usually administered to slaves, revolutionaries and criminals of the worst kind. So inhuman was crucifixion that the Emperor Constantine banned it around the year 315.

The first step in Jesus' crucifixion was a fierce scourging. This consisted of 39 or more lashes with a short leather whip tipped with sharp lead balls and sheep bones. It ripped into the flesh. An effective scourging would bring the helpless victim near death through blood loss, shock and excruciating pain. After a sleepless night, the emotional rigors of various trials across Jerusalem and the lack of sleep and food, Jesus would have been thoroughly drained of strength after a fierce scourging. Add to this a crown made of thick thorns, a prickly robe placed over the open wounds and the spittle of mocking guards and you can imagine the poor shape Jesus would have been as he walked to the site of the crucifixion.

Christians have traditionally honored Jesus by retracing the steps he walked to Calvary on Good Friday. This Way of the Cross, known as the Way of Sorrows (*Via Dolorosa*) stretched a third of a mile from the Fortress Antonia (where Jesus was sentenced) to Golgotha, the place of crucifixion. Jesus was so weak that Simon Cyrene, a visiting pilgrim to Jerusalem, was ordered to help Jesus carry the 125-pound crossbeam. Jesus fell several times, but he still comforted the women who were weeping for him.

When Jesus reached Golgotha, the soldiers tripped him to the ground. They used 5-inch iron nails to pound his wrists into the crossbeam. Four soldiers then hoisted him up onto the vertical beam (which was permanently anchored into the ground) and nailed his feet into a wooden foot rest.

Mark tells us that Jesus began his ordeal on the cross at 9 A.M. and died around 3 P.M. For those six hours he was plagued by mocking soldiers and gawking onlookers who badgered him to save himself. He was hung between two criminals, one of whom mercilessly insulted him. Beneath the cross was his mother, a beloved apostle and some faithful women disciples.

Sharp pains shot through his body as he grasped for breath. Insects buzzed around his open wounds. Parched lips longed for a drink as the body dehydrated. John's gospel reports that Jesus cried out, "I thirst." These were not Jesus' only words from the cross. The other gospels tell us that Jesus forgave his tormenters and gave his mother to the care of the beloved disciple, John. He also promised the "good thief" that he would have a place in paradise.

Most of those crucified died through suffocation. Their tired muscles could no longer support their bodies. The chest muscles would be stretched, and the victim could no longer exhale. Before his own death, which may have come from suffocation or perhaps heart failure due to intense shock, Jesus uttered the opening words of Psalm 22, "My God, my God, why have you deserted me?" If you read Psalm 22 to the end—a prayer Jesus undoubtedly completed silently—you will note that it proclaims God's ultimate mercy to his Suffering Servant. Far from a cry of despair, Psalm 22 is a prayer of supreme faith.

Luke's gospel tells us that Jesus died after committing himself to his Father. According to the Jewish way of marking time, evening was approaching and a new day was about to begin. Both the Sabbath and the Passover were about to begin at dusk, so the Jews felt a sense of urgency to get Jesus and the other two men into the grave. To hasten death, the soldiers typically broke the shin bones of crucified men. Their bodies would collapse and respiratory failure would swiftly bring death. However, when the soldiers got to Jesus, they found him already dead. To make sure, one of them pierced Jesus' side with a lance. Blood and water flowed out.

Joseph of Arimathea, a friend of Jesus and a member of the Sanhedrin, received permission to bury Jesus. After wrapping Jesus' body in a white shroud, he placed Jesus in a tomb hewn out of rock.

Jesus' suffering and death were over. A new age had begun. The gospels tell us that the Temple curtain in front of the Holy of Holies ripped in two. This symbolized the end of the old covenant and the beginning of a new covenant sealed in Jesus' blood. This covenant poured out on the cross heralded the remission of sin and everlasting life.

In the meantime, Jesus' followers were in a state of confusion and shock. Their master was gone! They withdrew

to a room in the city, grief-stricken and lost. After the holy days, the women would go to the tomb to anoint Jesus' hastily buried body.

Resurrection of Jesus.   Jesus' disciples were grieving when the women went to anoint Jesus' body on Easter Sunday morning. But their lives were about to change. They found the tomb empty! This did not *prove* to them that Jesus was alive; it only bewildered them. It was not until Jesus appeared to Mary Magdalene and the apostles that they became absolutely convinced that he was alive.

Consider the magnitude and importance of Jesus' resurrection from the dead. Nothing like it has ever happened in history before or after. *The person who claimed that he was the "resurrection and the life" is now alive.* After a cruel, brutal death because of his preaching and his loving life, Jesus the Lord rose from the dead! He lives among us.

So convinced were the early disciples that Jesus was alive that their lives were turned upside down. Because of the Holy Spirit descending on them on Easter/Pentecost, they changed from frightened sheep without a shepherd to bold witnesses. They left the upper room where they hovered in confusion to go out into the streets of Jerusalem and to the ends of the world to proclaim great news: Jesus of Nazareth lives! We have seen him! He has conquered death! He is the Messiah, the Lord, the Son of God! He has won for us our salvation, eternal life! Repent and believe!

Writing around A.D. 55, St. Paul presents the preaching about the risen Lord and lists those who saw him alive. This passage is an early Christian creed (statement of belief) about Jesus:

"[A] tradition which I had myself received, was that Christ died for our sins, in accordance with the scriptures, and that he was buried; and that on the third day, he was raised to life, in accordance with the scriptures; and that he appeared to Cephas; and later to the Twelve; and next he appeared to more than five hundred of the brothers at the same time, most of whom are still with us, though some have fallen asleep; then he appeared to James, and then to all the apostles. Last of all he appeared to me too" (1 Cor 15:3-8).

■ *journal* ■

Following is a list of all 12 appearances of Jesus recorded in the New Testament. Check out six of these references. In your journal, summarize what took place. Then, imagine yourself to be one of the persons to whom Jesus appeared. Write a few paragraphs describing the following:

a. What you feel about your Master now being alive

b. What he looks like

c. What he says to you

The Appearances:
    disciples on the road to Emmaus (Lk 24:13-35)
    the women (Mt 28:9-10)
    Mary Magdalene (Jn 20:11-18)
    Peter (Lk 24:34; 1 Cor 15:5)
    four separate appearances to the eleven and some other
        disciples (Jn 20:19-23; Jn 20:24-29; Mt 28:16-20; Acts
        1:6-9)
    seven disciples (Jn 21:1-14)
    more than five hundred brethren (1 Cor 15:6)
    James (1 Cor 15:7)
    Paul (Acts 9:3-8)

Jesus' resurrection proves that he is God. It has also won our own salvation. The resurrection is the central point of the gospel. St. Paul once again states the real significance of Jesus' rising,

> "If Christ has not been raised, then our preaching is without substance, and so is your faith" (1 Cor 15:14).

From the earliest days, though, nonbelievers challenged Christian belief in Jesus' resurrection. Some claimed that the apostles made up the story. However, what would they have to gain? First, no one in those early days could show that the empty tomb story was false. For example, no one could produce Jesus' body, and we can be sure that the opponents of the early Christians tried to do just that.

More important, many of the early Christians, including all the apostles except John, died for their conviction that Jesus lives. Who would be willing to suffer severe torture and death for a lie? The martyrdom of so many early Christians argues very strongly for the truth of Jesus' resurrection.

Some nonbelievers today claim that what the apostles did in telling the resurrection story was to show that Jesus' *message* lives on in the hearts of his followers. According to this theory, the apostles did not mean to speak *literally* of a resurrected body.

However, St. Paul emphatically states that Jesus was *seen* by the disciples. Thomas refused to believe until he saw the Lord who invited him to touch the wounds. Jesus even cooked some fish to show that he was real and not a ghost or some hallucination by the apostles.

Human reason has difficulty dealing with the resurrection. Philosophers through the ages have come up with five guesses on what takes place at death: (1) nothing—we cease to exist; (2) our soul lives on, but without a body; (3) we cease to exist as individuals—God absorbs us; (4) we become like a ghost—a pale half-survival condemned to misery; (5) reincarnation—we come back to earth in other bodies to try again.

The good news of Jesus' resurrection tells us that all these theories are false. Jesus' resurrected body was the same as, yet different from, his earthly body. It was so radically different—glorified—that even Mary Magdalene, Peter in the boat on the Sea of Galilee and the disciples at Emmaus had difficulty recognizing him. With the gift of faith given by the Holy Spirit, they did recognize their friend and Master as one alive! And they recognized him as infinitely great, as God's own Son, the Lord of the universe.

This is the faith of the resurrection. Jesus, our brother and Savior, is our Lord. His resurrection is the hope of our eternal life. He has ascended to the Father. In his glory, he reigns in heaven until he will come again at the end of the time. Yet, he mysteriously lives in the world—in his church, in his word, in the sacraments, in us—by the power of the Holy Spirit.

Jesus' resurrection gives us hope that our own death is birth into a glorious new life with God and our friends. If we have faith in the Lord and live as he commands us, then his destiny will be ours. We can only imagine what is in store:

> *What no eye has seen and no ear has heard, what the mind of man cannot visualize; all that God has prepared for those who love him* (1 Cor 2:9).

Living Jesus' Passion, Death and Resurrection

We call the mystery of Jesus' passion, death, resurrection and ascension/glorification the *paschal mystery*. The phrase paschal mystery refers to God's love demonstrated and communicated to us by Jesus our Savior.

Jesus' whole life communicates to us the nature of God's love for us. By freely entering into our human condition, riddled with sin and its effects, God's Son showed us how much we mean to him. The Incarnation—God becoming human in Jesus—is a supreme act of love on God's part. St. Paul shows the depths of that love when he writes:

> Who, being in the form of God,
> did not count equality with God
> something to be grasped.
>
> But he emptied himself,
> taking the form of a slave,
> becoming as human beings are;
> and being in every way like a human being,
> he was humbler yet,
> even to accepting death, death on a cross (Phil 2:6-8).

Through the Lord's sacrifice on the cross, he "passed over" from our sinful world to his Father. He was the Paschal Lamb (*paschal* means "passover") offered to the Father to atone for our sins. Jesus' resurrection is the Father's *yes* to his Son's offering his life. It completes the Passover. Thus, Jesus' death and resurrection together accomplish our salvation. They are the paschal mystery of God's love for us in his Son.

When we join ourselves to the Lord in faith and allow him to live in us, then we will be raised on the last day. This is his promise to us.

Imitating Jesus.   We can live the paschal mystery by living Jesus' cross and resurrection. We enter into Jesus' life at baptism where we die to sin and rise to a new life with him. Our baptism beckons us to renew ourselves daily and be reborn in the Holy Spirit. It reminds us to be faithful to our Lord. We do this when we daily carry the little crosses that come into our lives, for example, by enduring the pain and suffering involved in doing the right thing.

We celebrate Jesus' passover every time we participate at Mass. When we receive the Lord in the Eucharist, we join our Savior and partake in those deeds he accomplished for our salvation. The Eucharist reminds us to "be other Christs" by living as he did and sharing him with our fellow Christians and all people. The Eucharist tells us to break ourselves as Jesus did and give ourselves to others in loving and joyful service.

Before the Lord's ascension into heaven and his glorification at the right hand of the Father, he commanded us to continue his work here on earth:

> "All authority in heaven and on earth has been given to me. Go, therefore, make disciples of all nations; baptize them in the name of the Father and of the Son and of the Holy Spirit, and teach them to observe all the commands I gave you. And look, I am with you always; yes, to the end of time" (Mt 28:18-20).

We live the death and resurrection of Jesus when, in obedience, we try to live what the Lord commands us to do.

John's gospel shows us how we should live the paschal mystery. When Jesus appeared to the frightened apostles in the upper room on Easter Sunday, he gave them the Holy Spirit. The gift of the Holy Spirit unleashes God's power among us. Listen to Jesus' mandate:

> "As the Father sent me,
> so am I sending you" (Jn 20:21).

One sent by God is on a mission of the utmost importance. We Christians are missionaries empowered by the Holy Spirit to spread God's word and share his love with others.

We can show this love in a special way when we forgive others. Forgiveness calls for a death to our own grudges.

Its reward is a new life of union with the one we forgive. When we forgive, we love as Jesus did. Recall that he came to forgive us our sins so we can be reunited with God. We continue his work when we let go of the anger that divides us. Jesus shows that love unites and brings new life. The Christian imitates him.

Witnessing to the Lord

How well do you live the paschal mystery by witnessing to the Lord in word and deed? Check your performance in these areas. Mark according to this scale:

4 — I do this often
3 — I do this occasionally
2 — I do this rarely
1 — I never do this

_____ 1. I speak about my religious beliefs to others.

_____ 2. I forgive others when they wrong me.

_____ 3. I sacrifice small pleasures from time to time.

_____ 4. I speak the truth even when it hurts.

_____ 5. I endure setbacks with good cheer; I try to find value in every defeat.

_____ 6. I deny myself something in order to give to the poor.

_____ 7. I help people in need.

_____ 8. I defend those who are verbally abused by others.

_____ 9. I participate fully in the Mass and receive the Eucharist often.

_____ 10. I appreciate what the Lord has done for me and, as a result, am a joyful person.

■ *reflection* ■

Think of some concrete sacrifice you can make in the next week, for example, cutting out snacks to identify with the less fortunate. Take the money you save from doing this loving work and donate it to the missions.

■ *summary* ■

1. Jesus celebrated a Passover meal with his apostles on Holy Thursday in anticipation of his own sacrifice on the cross. He showed us the meaning of service at this meal and instituted the Holy Eucharist.

2. Jesus was arrested at night so his supporters could not defend him. The Jewish leaders saw Jesus as a threat to their religious views and influence over the people. They accused him of blasphemy. They presented him to Pilate as a political threat to Caesar, a crime punishable by death.

3. Jesus suffered the pain of scourging and crucifixion, a horrible form of the death penalty. Jesus freely surrendered his life for our salvation. In obedience he gave himself to his Father.

4. The resurrection of Jesus proves his divinity and assures us of eternal salvation. The various accounts all attest that Jesus lives, that he sends the Spirit to believers and that he reigns in heaven at the right hand of his Father.

Christ has died
Christ is risen
Christ will come again
　　—Memorial Acclamation

5. Jesus' resurrection tells us that our own death is a birth into a new life of a resurrected, glorified body in heaven for eternity.

6. We live the paschal mystery of Christ's redeeming actions when we sacrifice, forgive and love in imitation of the Lord.

7. Our baptism initiates us into the passion, death, resurrection and ascension of our Lord. The Eucharist commemorates and reenacts these sacred mysteries. At the Eucharist we receive the Risen Lord so we can take him into the world for other people.

▪ *focus questions* ▪

1. Explain the meaning of Jesus' washing the feet of his apostles at the Last Supper.

2. What did the various religious leaders have against Jesus? Why did they need someone like Judas?

3. Describe some of the major details of Jesus' trial, passion and crucifixion.

4. Give some evidences for the *reality* of Jesus' resurrection.

5. Name several people to whom Jesus appeared.

6. What are some of the theories about what happens to us at death? What do Christians believe about human destiny?

7. What is the *paschal mystery*? What does it mean for us to live the paschal mystery?

8. Identify and explain these terms:

Ascension	creed
blasphemy	resurrection
covenant	Sanhedrin

▪ *journal entries* ▪

1. Write a description of the crucifixion of Jesus from one of the following viewpoints:

Pilate	Mary Magdalene
Mary, his mother	the Roman centurion
Peter	Simon Cyrene
Caiaphas	the good thief

2. *Enriching your vocabulary.* Using a good dictionary, look up the meaning of the following words. Write the definitions in your journal.

adamant	passion
contemptuous	preliminary
glorify	respiratory
hallucination	shirk
manipulate	

Prayer Reflection

Down through the centuries, Christians have memorized and meditated on the "Seven Last Words of Jesus," that is, the seven last things he said from the cross. These words reveal his values and tell us about his suffering for us. Please pray these words of Jesus and reflect on their meaning.

1. **"Father, forgive them; they do not know what they are doing"** (Lk 23:34).

   Lord, grant me the strength to forgive those who have hurt me and don't understand me.

2. **"In truth I tell you, today you will be with me in paradise"** (Lk 23:43).

   Do I think to comfort others when they are hurting or lonely?

3. **"Woman, this is your son. . . . This is your mother"** (Jn 19:26-27).

   What good things have I done for *my* mother lately? Do I make her proud of me?

4. *"My God, my God, why have you forsaken me?"* (Mt 27:46).

   Read Psalm 22 in its entirety, a prayer that ends on a note of hope that God will rescue him. Do I have faith that God will be there for me when the going gets tough?

5. *"I am thirsty"* (Jn 19:28).

   Do I thirst for what is right? Or do I pursue false values?

6. **"It is fulfilled"** (Jn 19:30).

   Am I dependable? Do I follow through on my commitments?

7. **"Father, *into your hands I commit my spirit"*** (Lk 23:46).

   To what have I committed *my* spirit? Is God #1 in my life?

■ *resolution* ■

Memorize these words of Jesus.

chapter 9
Belief
Through
the Ages

He is the image of the unseen God,
the first-born of all creation,
for in him were created all things
in heaven and on earth:
everything visible and everything invisible . . .
He exists before all things
and in him all things hold together,
and he is the Head of the Body,
that is, the Church.

He is the Beginning,
the first-born from the dead.

—Colossians 1:15-16, 17-18.

In This Chapter

We will focus on:

- some important titles of Jesus
- Jesus of the councils
- Jesus of the Nicene Creed
- some questions about Jesus

Someone once remarked that the world contains three classes of people: the few who make things happen; the many who watch things happen; and the vast majority who have no idea of what happens. Today's world needs more people who make things happen.

Certainly Jesus made things happen. His death on the cross and his resurrection won eternal salvation for all people everywhere. No one has ever accomplished anything greater than this. Christians believe in Jesus and join themselves to him. They try to continue his ministry of love, worship and service. They join Jesus in making things happen.

Are you a Christian who makes things happen? If so, you belong to a Christian community of faith—the church—that has proclaimed the lordship of Jesus down through the centuries. Our calendar, which begins with Jesus' birth, announces that history revolves around him. Before his ascension into heaven, Jesus instructed his followers to spread his message throughout the world. Jesus is the message. Led by the Holy Spirit, Christians through the ages have told the world about the most amazing person who has ever lived: Jesus Christ!

Faith in Symbol

Many different symbols have illustrated Christian beliefs about Jesus down through the years. These symbols appear in religious paintings, in altar carvings in churches, on the walls of catacombs and in illustrations decorating Bibles. Most have a basis in a biblical quote or some traditional belief about Jesus.

Symbols are external signs of some reality. Words, for example, express ideas; they are external signs we can hear or see. Jesus is also a symbol, the perfect symbol of his Father. Jesus is God's own Word. He is a visible sign of the invisible God. Here are four common and important symbols of Jesus; all tell us something about our Christian faith in Jesus.

The Alpha and Omega.   Alpha is the first letter of the Greek alphabet; omega is the last letter. These letters symbolize that Jesus is the beginning and end of human history.

Lamb of God.   Jesus is the lamb of God, the innocent victim offered so that we might have eternal life. "Look, there is the lamb of God that takes away the sin of the world" (Jn 1:29).

Chi-Rho.   Chi and Rho are the first two letters of the Greek word for Christ. This common symbol for Jesus identifies him as the Messiah.

IXΘYΣ Fish. The Greek word *ichthus* means "fish." It is an anagram for the first letters of "Jesus Christ Son of God Savior."

I	—Iesous	= Jesus
X	—Christos	= Christ
Θ	—Theou	= of God
Y	—Uios	= Son
Σ	—Soter	= Savior

Your symbol. Draw a symbol to represent *your belief* about Jesus.

Titles of Jesus

You can tell a lot about people by the nicknames others give them. For example, you expect "The Brain" to be smart, "The Jock" to be a superior athlete and "The Knock-out" to be physically attractive.

The early Christians used certain titles when they preached Jesus to others. The New Testament reports many of these titles, which help us understand what Jesus did for us and who he is. They also shed light on what the early Christians believed about our Lord. We have already touched on some of the titles given to Jesus, for example, *Christ* (Messiah), the *New Moses*, the *Suffering Servant* and the *Word of God*, the Father's perfect self-communication.

The following titles of Jesus tell us something about what Christians believe about Jesus.

Lord. During his earthly ministry, people sometimes addressed Jesus as lord, an address that meant sir or master and signaled respect. After Pentecost, Christians gave him this title to stress that he was lord or ruler of the universe.

Closely associated with this idea was the belief that only God was Lord of all creation. To call Jesus Lord affirms that he is God. It was the earliest title used after the resurrection to indicate the *divinity* of Jesus, the Christ. Paul proclaims time and again the most ancient of all Christian creeds—Jesus Christ is Lord!

Son of God. This title designates Jesus' true identity. When Jesus approached Peter during the storm at sea, walking across the water, Peter, awe-struck, proclaimed: "Truly, you are the Son of God." This faith statement reflects Christian belief about Jesus as God-made-flesh. Jesus is God's only son, our loving God's gift to us. Later Christian reflection teaches that God's Son is the Second Person of the Blessed Trinity.

Prophet. This title underscores Jesus' role as one who testifies to the truth. Jesus told Pilate, "I came into the world for this, to bear witness to the truth" (Jn 18:37). It takes courage to be a prophet. Speaking the truth is difficult, especially when someone is threatening your life. Jesus—like so many prophets before and after him—was put to death because the authorities did not want to hear the truth. His courage to preach God's word inspires us to be on his side, the side of truth and justice.

High Priest. A priest is a mediator between God and people, a go-between. Because of Adam and Eve's sin, a gulf between God and his creatures had opened. God appointed priests, anointed to perform their task of offering sacrifice, to help bridge the gap between God and his people.

Jesus is the High Priest who gave himself as the perfect sacrifice.

> But now Christ has come, as the high priest of all the blessings which were to come. . . . he has entered the sanctuary once and for all, taking with him not the blood of goats and bull calves, but his own blood, having won an eternal redemption (Hb 9:11-12).

Jesus has united us with his Father, and by his sacrifice has atoned for our sins. He has brought us into union with the source of life.

King. Jesus, the King of the Universe, rules at God's right hand. During his earthly ministry he rejected a kingdom of domination and control of others. He taught that greatness in his kingdom lies in serving others, not in lording it over them. The sign of his kingdom is love.

Jesus' rule, marked by peace and justice, will be perfectly realized at the end of time. Then, everyone will recognize him as the Lord of heaven and earth. In the meantime he commands his followers to work for his kingdom.

Our baptism enables us to share in Jesus' prophetic, priestly and kingly ministry. When we proclaim the gospel in truth and with courage, we imitate Jesus the prophet. When we live virtuous lives that attract others to God, we share in his priestly ministry. And when we promote God's reign through acts of loving service, we partake in his kingship.

Other Titles

The New Testament gives us many titles of Jesus. Look up the appropriate scriptural reference for each title below and briefly state what each means. In your journal, note your favorite title of Jesus and write a brief paragraph discussing why you like this title.

> **Good Shepherd** (Jn 10:11)
>
> **Living Water** (Jn 4:14)
>
> **Bread of Life** (Jn 6:35)
>
> **Light of the World** (Jn 1:4,5,9)
>
> **Divine Physician** (Mt 9:12-13)
>
> **Judge** (Acts 17:31)

Jesus of the Councils

Belief about Jesus—who he is and his meaning for us—has developed through the ages. People are inquisitive; they ask questions and want answers. Sometimes the answers they pose go against what the early church and the apostles both believed and taught about Jesus. In these cases, the church must clarify its teaching and present it so Christians and others clearly understand what we believe about Jesus and the salvation he has won for us.

Catholics hold that Jesus lives in the church. He promised that he would be with us always. Jesus leads and guides us through the power of the Holy Spirit. He appointed Peter, the apostles and their successors—the pope and bishops—as leaders to help guide the church. These Christ-appointed teachers state and clarify exactly what we believe.

Through history, the pope and bishops have met in worldwide ecumenical councils to discuss, reflect on and teach Catholic beliefs. The early councils of the church addressed some of the more serious challenges to the traditional beliefs about Jesus. The chart on pages 173-174 outlines these heresies and summarizes what the church teaches about Jesus.

The Conflict: Jesus—Both God and Man?   The history of the controversies concerning teaching about Jesus is both fascinating and complex. The controversies resulted when Jesus was preached to people immersed in Greek philosophy. They tried to interpret Jesus in a different way than the apostles understood him.

One group of false teachings—*Docetism*—held that Jesus only *seemed* to be a man. This heresy taught that though Jesus' body appeared real, it was only an illusion. The Docetists *denied Jesus' humanity* because they could not imagine how the eternal God could possibly hunger, thirst, suffer and die for us. To be human seemed so ungodly. This view denied the death and resurrection of Jesus. If this were true, then our salvation is an illusion, too.

On the other extreme, Arius—a priest from Alexandria in Egypt—denied Jesus' equality with God. He accepted that Jesus was God's greatest creature, but Arius claimed that Jesus was not divine and thus was not equal to God. A later heretic, Theodore of Mopsuestia, so stressed the humanity of Jesus that he ended up denying his divinity. Like Docetism, *Arianism* also seriously challenges the heart of our religion. If Jesus is not truly God, by what power and authority does he redeem us from our sins? Our salvation is lost.

At the Council of Nicea (325), the bishops issued a *creed*, or profession of faith, asserting that Jesus was *both* God and human. The Council of Constantinople (381) restated this creed and also taught that Jesus has a human soul. We recite this profession of faith, the Nicene-Constantinopolitan Creed, at Mass today.

How Many Persons in Christ?   A later problem concerning Jesus dealt with the number of persons in Christ. Nestorius falsely taught that Jesus was both a divine person and a human person. He claimed that Mary was only the mother of the human Jesus. The Council of Ephesus (431) condemned Nestorius. It taught that Jesus is *one* person—a divine person—and thus it is appropriate to call Mary the Mother of God. We worship *one* Christ and Lord, not a human being along with the divine Word.

Eutyches made a different error. He maintained that Jesus' human nature was absorbed into his divine nature. Thus, he taught that Jesus only had a divine nature.

The Council of Chalcedon (451) corrected this false view by teaching that Jesus was *one divine person with both a divine nature and a human nature.* This statement, known as the *Chalcedon formula,* summarizes the classic teaching of the church about Jesus. The Second Council of Constantinople (553) confirmed this teaching. A final early council (the Third Council of Constantinople, 680-1) taught that since Jesus had two natures, he also possessed two wills. Jesus' human will, though distinct from his divine will, was not opposed to it.

Church Teaching in Brief.   In summary, the church teaches *who* Jesus is—he is *one person,* the Second Person of the Trinity. He is one divine person, equal to God. He is the Word-made-flesh.

The church also teaches that Jesus has two natures. This means he exists both as God and as a human being. He can do what humans do, but because he is a divine person, he can also do what God does. No one else exists as Jesus does. He is unique. In Jesus, God truly becomes *what human beings are* while *remaining what God is;* Jesus is truly God-made-human.

Jesus is the Second Person of the Trinity . . . one divine person, equal to God . . . the Word-made flesh.

What the Early Councils Teach About Jesus

The Council	Church Teaching	The Heresy
Nicea (325)	Jesus is "consubstantial" with the Father; he is divine.	*Arianism:* Jesus is only a creature, not equal to the Father.

Ephesus (431)	Jesus is *one* person, a *divine* person. Mary is truly the "Mother of God."	*Nestorianism*: Jesus was two persons —one human and one divine.
Chalcedon (451)	Jesus is both human and divine.	*Docetism*: Jesus' body was only an illusion. God did not really become one of us.
	He is *one divine person* with both a *divine nature* and a *human nature*.	*Monophysitism*: (meaning "one nature" in the Greek) Jesus only has a divine nature.

The Jesus of the Creed

Let us turn to the classic statement of faith in Jesus, the Nicene Creed, and analyze what it teaches. We recite it every Sunday at Mass.

We believe in one God, the Father, the Almighty, maker of heaven and earth, of all that is seen and unseen.

Our God is almighty and all powerful, perfectly one, the creator of everything that is. Yet, our all-powerful God is our loving *Abba*, whom we can address with great trust. God loves us beyond what we can possibly imagine.

We believe in one Lord, Jesus Christ, the only Son of God, eternally begotten of the Father, God from God, Light from Light, true God from true God, begotten, not made, one in Being with the Father. Through him all things were made.

God so loves us that he proves his love through his Son, Jesus, through whom all things were made. This passage affirms that Jesus is both divine and the Lord of creation. He always existed as God's only Son. Jesus is indeed the Lord.

For us and for our salvation he came down from heaven:

Jesus came to save us from our sins. His mission was to heal the alienation caused by Adam's sin, an alienation that separates us from God, other people and ourselves. Jesus is God's gift to us to rescue us from death and bring us home to heaven.

By the power of the Holy Spirit he was born of the Virgin Mary, and became man.

The mystery of the Incarnation—God becoming human in Jesus—took place because a young girl, Mary, said yes to God. Her faith in God's power to do marvelous things is an example for us today. The doctrine of the Incarnation underscores that Jesus was truly human.

Jesus' conception by God's Spirit means that God's gracious activity brings forth our salvation. Jesus represents a new beginning of the human race, a beginning started by God, not by us.

For our sake he was crucified under Pontius Pilate; he suffered, died, and was buried.

Jesus' preaching of God's reign and his call to people to conversion led to resistance and misunderstanding. Jesus did not give up, though. In an act of love and obedience to God and redemptive love *for us,* Jesus freely surrendered himself on the cross. He underwent a terrible death for our sake.

On the third day he rose again in fulfillment of the Scriptures;

This faith statement proclaims that Jesus is alive! Through his life, death *and* resurrection, Jesus has conquered sin and death. He has redeemed us from slavery to sin and the devil. His resurrection is the source of our own hope for eternal life.

He ascended into heaven and is seated at the right hand of the Father. He will come again in glory to judge the living and the dead, and his kingdom will have no end.

This clause of the creed affirms that the risen Lord now lives with God. He intercedes for us, his brothers and sisters, at God's "right hand," a privileged position of special honor and influence. We also believe that one day in the future God's reign will be fully established throughout the universe. Jesus' good news, his person and his message, will serve as the standard to judge all creatures. One day all creation will acknowledge the central fact of our faith: Jesus Christ is Lord!

We believe in the Holy Spirit, the Lord, the giver of life, who proceeds from the Father and the Son. With the Father and the Son he is worshiped and glorified. He has spoken through the Prophets.

Here we profess that the Holy Spirit, the source of our life and gifts, is a member of the Blessed Trinity. The Spirit's role in relationship to us and Jesus is to empower us to recognize and believe in Jesus. The Holy Spirit dwells in us and directs our hearts and minds to Jesus who draws us to God. The Holy Spirit helps us, the members of Christ's body, to continue the Lord's work until he comes in glory.

We believe in one holy catholic and apostolic Church. We acknowledge one baptism for the forgiveness of sins. We look for the resurrection of the dead and the life of the world to come.

In the final passage of the Creed, we acknowledge that Jesus lives in the church. We take seriously his command to baptize in the name of the Father, Son and Spirit. When we profess our belief in the resurrection, we acknowledge that Jesus' own resurrection is the source of our eternal happiness. We look to everlasting life because of our Savior and Lord Jesus Christ.

- *resolution* -

Memorize the Creed.

The Many-Sided Jesus

Listed below are some of the ways people have understood Jesus through the ages. For each pair, mark with an X the place on the continuum which most expresses your belief about Jesus.

Jesus will judge us at the end of time	_____	Jesus accepts everyone and rejects no one
Jesus is our almighty God	_____	Jesus is our brother
Jesus hates sin, especially hypocrisy	_____	Jesus forgives everything

Jesus deserves our   ——————   Jesus is our friend
worship

Jesus sits at the right   ——————   Jesus dwells in the
hand of God in   hearts of his
heaven   disciples

▪ *discuss* ▪

Why did you mark each pair as you did?

Find scriptural quotes to support the view of Jesus most attractive to you.

Two Questions About Jesus

There has been no major doctrinal development on Jesus since the teaching of the early councils. Later councils usually repeated what the earlier councils taught.

Here are a couple of popular questions people ask about Jesus.

Did Jesus Have Brothers and Sisters? As more and more people read the Bible on their own, they begin to notice passages like Matthew 12:46, John 2:12 and Acts 1:14 which mention certain "brothers" of Jesus. Mark 6:2-3 even mentions four of them by name: James, Joset, Jude and Simon. Mark also refers to certain sisters of Jesus.

Although some Protestants have no difficulty accepting this at face value, Catholics have always held to the virginity of Mary. We believe that Jesus was born of a virgin and that Mary always remained a virgin. Both infancy narratives in Matthew and Luke support this tradition. They believed, as do Catholics, that Jesus is both God (conceived by the power of the Holy Spirit) and human (born of Mary). Mary's lifelong virginity is a sign of her exclusive dedication to God's will and to her unique son, Jesus.

Brother and *sister* (*adelphos* in the Greek) could mean relative or kinsman or cousin. Jesus' era was the time of an extended or patriarchal family. The oldest living male—the patriarch—was considered the father of the family, and all the relatives of the larger family were considered brothers and sisters. These relatives of Jesus, probably his cousins, grew up in Nazareth with him.

▪ *journal* ▪

Using the Nicene Creed as a guide, write up your own creed to express your beliefs about Jesus. Use symbols, pictures and other artwork to illustrate this creed. Be prepared to share it with your classmates.

Scripture supports this view. For example, the James and Joset mentioned above could not be the sons of Mary, Jesus' mother. Matthew (27:56) and Mark (15:40) mention them as sons of another Mary. She was one of the women who came to see Jesus crucified and who went to anoint Jesus on Easter morning. Furthermore, if Jesus had blood brothers, why would Jesus have entrusted his mother to John, the beloved disciple, and not to one of his brothers? (See Jn 19:26).

Who Is Responsible for Jesus' Death?   This question crops up because even today people sometimes wish to blame the Jewish people—God's Chosen People—for Jesus' death. A truly sad chapter in Christian history has been the attitude that the Jews as a nation should be held responsible for rejecting the Messiah. This attitude, found first even in Matthew's gospel (Mt 27:25), was repeated by some of the early church fathers. It has justified prejudice and many atrocities committed against the Jews throughout the centuries.

Blaming the Jews for the Black Death, confining them to ghettos, restricting their civil liberties and many other crimes against them were common in the Middle Ages. In our own century the dictator Adolf Hitler engineered the Holocaust. This gross attempt to eliminate the Jewish people was allowed to happen because of many centuries of Christian persecution against Jesus' own people.

The question of Jewish guilt for Jesus' death has been an intense issue in our century. At the Second Vatican Council, the bishops issued a strong statement removing any basis for anti-Semitism, hatred against the Jews:

> What happened in His passion cannot be blamed upon all the Jews then living, without distinction, nor upon the Jews of today. . . . The Jews should not be presented as repudiated or cursed by God.
>
> The Church . . . deplores the hatred, persecutions, and displays of anti-Semitism directed against Jews at any time and from any source (*Declaration on the Relationship of the Church to Non-Christian Religions*, No. 4).

Hatred and prejudice against the Jews or any other people is against everything Jesus taught and died for. Christians abhor prejudice in any form. Pontius Pilate, a Roman governor, pronounced the death sentence on Jesus. Some of the religious leaders saw Jesus as a threat and wished to remove him from the scene. So they brought Jesus to trial. But Jesus' own people were no more guilty of his death than we are. Christians know that sin brought about Jesus' death — the sin of all people from all times. Jesus did not flee from his death, but embraced it freely to accomplish our salvation. So much is his love for us.

Love Your Enemy

Jesus taught by his words and example that we must love everyone as our brother or sister. When God became one with us in Jesus, God took all of us into his loving embrace. God loves everyone. Followers of Jesus know that we cannot say we love God if we cannot love our neighbors.

Yet, prejudice is like a cancer eating away at our society. We prejudge someone without examining all the evidence. Jesus wants us to examine the truth that other people are our brothers and sisters. Examine how loving you are by marking the following. Then, please discuss the questions that follow.

Am I someone who . . .

1. is offended when someone makes a negative remark about the Jews?   Yes   No

2. believes it is wrong to make ethnic jokes?   Yes   No

3. believes it is wrong to laugh at ethnic jokes?   Yes   No

4. would approve of interracial marriages?   Yes   No

5. defends people who are the victims of prejudice?   Yes   No

6. makes friends with others regardless of what others may think?   Yes   No

7. thinks prejudice is a sin and would confess it as such in the sacrament of reconciliation?   Yes   No

▪ *discuss* ▪

1. Discuss the forms of prejudice in evidence in your school. What is the worst kind? What things can you and your classmates do to help overcome prejudice?

2. Is prejudice against Jews a problem in our country? Explain. Find examples in news magazines, television specials, the daily paper and the like of recent outbreaks of prejudice directed at racial, ethnic or religious groups. Is prejudice against women a reality in the world today? Is it common or an exception? Explain your response.

3. Find several teachings of Jesus that would indicate that prejudice is sinful and against his message.

▪ *summary* ▪

1. The titles of Jesus reveal his identity and show Christian faith in him. *Lord* stresses that Jesus is God. *Son of God* shows his intimate relationship with the Father.

2. Jesus as *Prophet* speaks the truth on God's behalf. Jesus the *High Priest* offers himself as a perfect sacrifice to the Father and bridges the gap separating us from God. Jesus the *King* teaches that leadership means service.

3. The early councils of the church had to fight two major false beliefs about Jesus. The first—Docetism—denied Jesus' humanity; it held that Jesus only appeared to be a man. The second—Arianism—denied Jesus' divinity. Arius taught that Jesus was God's greatest creature, but that he was not equal to the Father.

4. The church's teaching about Jesus is summed up in the *Chalcedon formula*: Jesus is one divine person with two natures (a divine nature and a human nature).

5. The Nicene Creed summarizes traditional Catholic faith in God the Father, Son and Holy Spirit. The doctrine of the Incarnation affirms both Jesus' divinity and his humanity. The creed also professes Jesus' virgin birth and his saving role. It proclaims the paschal mystery of love which won our eternal life. It states that Jesus has sent the Spirit to abide in us and his holy church.

6. Mary, the Mother of God, was always a virgin. Jesus' so-called "brothers and sisters" were probably his cousins.

7. Anti-Semitism, and all prejudice, is contrary to Jesus' gospel. The church teaches that the entire Jewish people cannot be held responsible for Jesus' death. Pilate condemned Jesus after some Jewish leaders handed him over.

▪ *focus questions* ▪

1. Discuss the meaning and significance of any four titles of Jesus.

2. Why did the church have to clarify its teaching and belief about Jesus?

3. Identify the following: Arianism, Docetism and the Chalcedon formula.

4. What does it mean when we say Jesus has a divine nature? a human nature?

5. Recite from memory the Nicene Creed.

6. Did Jesus have any brothers or sisters? Explain.

7. Define the term *anti-Semitism*. Why is it wrong?

▪ *journal entries* ▪

1. *Being prophet, priest, king:* The Holy Spirit empowers all Christians to share in Jesus' ministry. The Spirit calls us to be servants of truth (prophets), mediation (priests) and service (kings). How about you?

    In your journal, construct three lists that answer the following:

    a. ways I can serve the truth.
    b. ways I can bring God to others.
    c. ways I can serve others.

    Select several items from each list and check your performance (from 5 — *excellent* to 1 — *poor*).

2. *Enriching your vocabulary.* Using a good dictionary, look up the meaning of the following terms. Write the definitions in your journal.

> ghetto
> holocaust
> shackle

■ *class project* ■

Bring your lists from journal entry #1 to class and share them. As a class devise one service project and implement it during the next couple of weeks. It will be a wonderful way to put your faith in Jesus in practice as you near the end of the course.

Prayer Reflection

"I am the bread of life.
No one who comes to me will ever hunger;
no one who believes in me will ever thirst. . . .
I am the living bread which has come down from
    heaven.
Anyone who eats this bread will live for ever;
and the bread that I shall give
is my flesh, for the life of the world."

—John 6:35, 51

■ *reflection* ■

What three things do you really hunger for in life right now? How might the Lord satisfy these hungers?

■ *resolution* ■

Go to Mass one extra time this week and receive our Lord in holy communion. Ask him to take care of your true needs. Thank him for all he has given to you.

chapter 10

Jesus and You

Meeting the Risen Lord

God has sent into our hearts the Spirit of his Son crying, "*Abba*, Father"; and so you are no longer a slave, but a son; and if a son, then an heir, by God's own act.

—Galatians 4:6-7

Before his ascension into heaven, Jesus instructed his disciples to go into the world to continue his work. He promised to be with them always, until the end of time. Jesus expects his disciples to be missionaries, to be ambassadors for him and his Father.

But Jesus also reminds us that he is always available to us, to nourish and give us strength:

> "Come to me, all you who labor and are overburdened, and I will give you rest. Shoulder my yoke and learn from me, for I am gentle and humble in heart, *and you will find rest for your souls.* Yes, my yoke is easy and my burden light" (Mt 11:28-30).

Jesus invites us to come to him and be both his friend and disciple. The payoff is great. He is the source of our every happiness.

Jesus cares about you. He will not leave you. You have his word on it. He wants you to seek him out in your everyday life. Why? Because he needs you to continue his work. He wants you to be his light for others.

Jesus and You

The quote that opens this chapter reminds us that our Lord has sent his Holy Spirit to live in us. By the power of the Holy Spirit, we are adopted into God's family. Everyone becomes our sister or brother in Christ. As members of God's family, we have the privilege of helping to spread the good news of our true relationship to God.

185

The Holy Spirit gives us gifts to help continue the Lord's work on earth. St. Paul lists some of these in 1 Corinthians 12. They include preaching with wisdom, instruction, faith, healing, miracles, prophecy, recognizing spirits, speaking in tongues and interpreting tongues. The greatest gift of all, though, is love.

Read 1 Corinthians 12.   Try to identify *your* greatest gift. What is special about you? What quality do you have that helps others meet Jesus Christ? Here are some possibilities. Check off those that pertain to you. Add a couple others to the list. Share your choices with a classmate and explain how you have used these gifts to be "light of the world."

_____ joyful   _____ thoughtful   _____ generous

_____ helpful   _____ forgiving   _____ intelligent

_____ accepting   _____ gentle   _____ courageous

_____ patient

• *journal* •

Write a few paragraphs describing a time when you felt God using you to help draw others to him. You might also compose a short prayer of thanksgiving to the Lord for the many gifts he has given to you.

Jesus Lives in You

Jesus lives in you! This earth-shaking statement sums up an important aspect of the gospel. So precious are you in God's eyes that his Son Jesus, our risen Lord, has chosen to be present in the world through his disciples. Read the words of Jesus speaking to you and to all people of faith:

> "I am the true vine,
> and my Father is the vinedresser. . . .
> Remain in me, as I in you. . . .
> I am the vine,
> you are the branches.
> Whoever remains in me, with me in him,
> bears fruit in plenty. . . .
> If you remain in me
> and my words remain in you,
> you may ask for whatever you please
> and you will get it" (Jn 15:1, 4-5, 7).

At baptism we join the Christian community of faith. We become members of Christ's body and temples of the Holy Spirit. Christians have immense dignity because our Lord has chosen to be present in today's world through us. Christ lives in us. St. Paul reminds us of this truth:

> "I have been crucified with Christ and yet I am alive; yet it is no longer I, but Christ living in me. The life that I am now living . . . I am living in faith, faith in the Son of God who loved me and gave himself for me" (Gal 2:19-20).

St. Paul said we need faith to appreciate Christ's life in us. *Faith* is an important Christian virtue. It is a *kind of vision*, a way of seeing the true nature of things. It is a *response to Jesus' invitation to love.*

St. Teresa of Avila, a great spiritual writer, emphasized that the Christian has the hands of Christ to heal those who are hurting, the feet of Christ to walk to those in need, the eyes of Christ to search out the suffering, the voice of Christ to proclaim the good news. This Christian is *you.*

Someone once wrote, "I wondered why somebody didn't do something for peace; then I realized I am somebody." With Christ living in us, everybody is somebody. But this also means that we have the responsibility to be Christs for others. Consider the power we have. Jesus is on our side. At the Last Supper, he prayed:

> "I pray not only for these
> but also for those
> who through their teaching will come to believe in
>   me.
> May they all be one,
> just as, Father, you are in me and I am in you,
> so that they also may be in us,
> so that the world may believe it was you who sent
>   me" (Jn 17:20-21).

Faith is the "confident assurance concerning what we hope for, and conviction about things we do not see" (Heb 11:1, *New American Bible*).

Jesus Lives in the Church

The Christian Community.   Jesus set up the church to continue his saving mission. During his earthly ministry, he formed his disciples to learn and share the message that he was the way, the truth and the life. After his resurrection, he sent his Spirit to empower his followers to continue his work. Moreover, he promised to be with them until the end of time, promising: "Where two or three meet in my name, I am there among them'' (Mt 18:20).

Vatican II teaches how Jesus is present to us in the church:

> Christ, having been lifted up from the earth, is draw-ing all men to Himself (Jn 12:32). Rising from the dead (cf. Rom 6:9), He sent His life-giving Spirit upon His disciples and through this Spirit has established His body, the Church, as the universal sacrament of sal-vation. Sitting at the right hand of the Father, he is continually active in the world, leading men to the Church, and through her joining them more closely to Himself and making them partakers of His glorious life by nourishing them with His own body and blood (*Dogmatic Constitution on the Church*, #48).

The church is the *body of Christ*. He is the head, we are the members. Baptism incorporates us into the body. Each of us must use our talents to build up the body and con-tinue Jesus' work of salvation and sanctification in the world. The church—made up of people like us—continues Christ's work. We do it when we . . .

(1) *proclaim* his message of love and forgiveness;

(2) *build community* among our fellow believers;

(3) *serve others*, especially those who most need our words and deeds of compassion.

▪ *list making* ▪

As a class compose a list of five ways you and your class-mates can accomplish each of the three tasks mentioned above. Construct lists for each of the following categories of people:

- a. your families
- b. your classmates
- c. people in your community

Saints.   As members of Christ's body, Jesus sends to us heroic men and women to inspire us to follow him more faithfully. They take seriously Jesus' challenge to love. We call these models of holiness saints.

Each of us looks to personal Christian heroes to inspire us on our Christian journey. However, one Christian saint outshines them all as model of a true disciple of Jesus— Mary, the Mother of God, the supreme model of holiness. Mary's life witnesses to true holiness. Her entire life of faith in her Son is a model to us all.

Jesus wants us all to be saints, holy ones he calls apart to do his work. However, the church officially recognizes certain people who have cultivated a deep friendship with the Lord, a friendship so strong that Christ shines through their lives. The way they live shows us how real people can put their faith into practice.

In addition to these well-known saints, people close to you may well be the unsung heroes whose lives are worth imitating. Can you see Christ in the love of your mother and father, in their care and concern for you? Can you see Jesus through your teachers, training your mind so you can one day help others more effectively? Do you see the Lord in the person who rides on the same bus with you? Do you see the face of Jesus in everyone who comes into your life? He is there. We need only look.

The Christian always remembers that he or she is also Christ. The Lord has chosen each of us to be his ambassador, his missionary of love. He comes into the world through us. His love touches others when we love.

Sacraments

Jesus is present to us through sacred signs. The sacraments are visible signs of his care and love for us. They are concrete symbols of love.

Jesus takes seriously our humanity. Being human means having a body, being in touch with the material world. When the Word became flesh, God made holy the human body and all created reality.

Jesus ate with people, walked with them, laughed at their jokes, cried when his friends died. He showed his love by touching the sick, by taking children into his lap, by suffering a cruel passion and death. We know love when we experience it through gestures, embraces, symbols and words. We need signs because we are human.

Jesus instituted the sacraments so we can stay in touch with him. They are material symbols—using words, actions and concrete signs—to express the love, concern, forgiveness and real presence of the Lord. Through them and in them Jesus meets us and touches our hearts. When we celebrate the sacraments attentively we can sense the peace and joy Jesus has in store for us in his heavenly kingdom.

In *baptism*, for example, our Lord extends to us the invitation and privilege to join his body, the church. Through the presence and concern of other Christians, he promises to support us on our life's journey to God. *Confirmation* strengthens our faith commitment by showering on us the gifts of the Spirit. In the sacrament of *matrimony* the Lord joins a couple as they begin an exciting but difficult vocation. He promises to be with them in their lovemaking, in their daily struggles to be faithful, in the trials that inevitably come. In *holy orders* the Lord is present to the Christian community through special ministers who serve the church and lead it in worship. In the sacrament of the *anointing of the sick* Jesus sustains us spiritually and sometimes heals us physically. He meets us in many of the key events of our life—at birth, in sickness, when we need adult strength to live out his mandate to love others, when we choose a state in life.

We also appreciate meeting Jesus in two sacraments that are available to us as often as we choose to celebrate them—reconciliation and the Eucharist.

Reconciliation is an important way to meet Jesus and receive his healing touch of forgiveness. Today's emphasis in the sacrament is on reconciliation with the Christian community. When we sin we have harmed our relationship with God and with others. From time to time, especially when we have sinned seriously, we need to ask for God's pardon. We need to express our sorrow, experience the reassurance of our Lord's forgiveness and heal any wounds we have caused in Christ's body. Many Catholics find a caring, loving, sensitive Jesus in this sacrament. They find a Jesus who accepts them in their weakness and gives them the strength to try again to live the vocation of love that he has bestowed on them.

In many ways the *Eucharist* is the most important of the sacraments. It both celebrates and creates Christian community. It reenacts the paschal mystery of God's incredible love for us in Jesus. It reminds us to be Christ for others, to be "bread for the world."

Catholics believe that Jesus is truly present, body and blood, in the bread and wine consecrated in the eucharistic liturgy (the Mass). When we receive holy communion, we receive the Lord himself. The Eucharist is our greatest source of strength and nourishment as Christians. We receive the Lord who transforms us, living in us as we meet and serve people in our daily life. We receive Jesus not to keep him to ourselves but to let him shine through us as we become "light of the world" and "salt of the earth."

Jesus is also present in the eucharistic celebration in the priest who leads us in worship. He is present in our brothers and sisters who come to celebrate what Jesus has done for us. He is present, in addition, in the reading of the word that reminds us of the saving deeds God has accomplished for us.

Bread of Life

Please read John 6. Jesus calls himself the bread of life. He has come to fill our every need. Rate how you look to the Lord for his help and nourishment according to this scale:

      1 — This describes me well
      2 — I need improvement
      3 — I have a lot of work to do on this item

_____ **Scripture:** I read the Bible to see what God wants of me.

_____ **Eucharist:** I participate fully in the Mass at least once a week.

_____ **Fasting:** I deny myself something that I want to build up my spiritual body.

_____ **Prayer:** I turn to the Lord for help when I need it and to thank him for the times he came through for me.

_____ **Bread for others:**   As the Lord is a source of life for me, I try to be bread for others. For example, I share money with the poor. Or I listen compassionately to a lonely classmate who needs me.

Scripture—God's Word

One way to look at the Bible is to see it as "words of the Word." The gospels contain many teachings of Jesus, teachings that can touch us and change our lives. Think of the sacred scriptures as love letters sent to us from the one who loves us most. We won't profit from the letters unless we read them; they are of little value if left unopened and unread. However reading the word of God touches and transforms us. God's word is a powerful sign of his presence and love.

Faithful followers of Jesus will read scripture quietly, slowly and reflectively. Convinced that the risen Lord meets us in his holy word, we cannot remain the same if we read the Bible on a regular basis. The great missionary to Africa, David Livingstone sums it up well: "All that I am I owe to Jesus Christ, revealed to me in his divine book."

Meeting Jesus in Prayer

To experience Jesus as a friend means that we must spend time with him. All friendships are built on communication and availability. Friends are open to each other and try to get to know one another. Prayer is an important means Christians use to get close to Jesus.

Prayer is talking to God, spending time with him, noticing his presence, allowing him to contact us and come into our lives. Simply talking to Jesus as our closest, most understanding friend can be the best prayer of all. It is a marvelous way to meet the Lord.

Four traditional forms of prayer are **vocal** prayers, which are expressed in either your own words or those of another; **meditation**, which is thinking about some aspect of God and his meaning for you; **affective** prayer, which involves your feelings and imagination; and **contemplation,** which is resting in the Lord's presence, not thinking about anything in particular but simply enjoying God's company.

Jesus is truly involved in your life. When you reflect on the people you have met and the events that have happened to you, you might be able to see the Lord working through them. At night before going to sleep, try examining your day in the presence of Jesus. Ask him to show you the good you have done. Thank him for all those things. Also examine how you did not live as his brother or sister. Ask his forgiveness and resolve to improve tomorrow.

We can pray anytime and anywhere. However, it is a good idea to have a special time (for example, in the morning or in the evening) and a special place for conversing with the Lord.

Prayer can be tough. Distractions will inevitably come our way. But merely attempting to pray, trying to meet the Lord, is itself a prayer. No one who prays is left unchanged. The Lord will meet you if you want him to. He will enable you to love others as he loves you. It is worth the effort.

Jesus on Prayer

Here are some of Jesus' most famous words on prayer. Reflect on them carefully. Judge your own faith response to them.

> 1 — I firmly believe this
> 2 — I want to believe this
> 3 — I'm not sure this is true

_____ 1. "In your prayers do not babble as the gentiles do, for they think that by using many words they will make themselves heard" (Mt 6:7).

_____ 2. "So I say to you: Ask, and it will be given to you; search, and you will find; knock, and the door will be opened to you" (Lk 11:9).

_____ 3. "For everyone who raises himself up will be humbled, but anyone who humbles himself will be raised up" (Lk 18:14).

■ *discuss* ■

When has prayer helped you?

Jesus Lives in Others

If you want to see what Jesus looks like in today's world, look in the mirror. Then, turn to your neighbors and picture Jesus in them also. With the eyes of faith, the Holy Spirit enables us to see that we are God's adopted children. We are brothers and sisters of Jesus and, in him, brothers and sisters of one another. Jesus emphatically taught that love of God and love of neighbor are inseparable:

> *"You must love the Lord your God with all your heart, with all your soul,* with all your mind *and with all your strength. . . . You must love your neighbor as yourself"* (Mk 12:30-31).

To love Jesus means simply that we must love everyone he loves. The message of the parable of the Good Samaritan is that everyone, even our enemy, is our neighbor. Each person has tremendous dignity and is worthy of our love and respect. Jesus says we cannot love the invisible God if we fail to love the person we can see.

In a special way, Jesus identified himself with the lowly, the outcast, those who were not accepted by the well-established. He taught that we will be judged by how we welcome the stranger, feed the hungry, give drink to the thirsty, visit the sick and the imprisoned.

> "In truth I tell you, in so far as you neglected to do this to one of the least of these, you neglected to do it to me" (Mt 25:45).

We *must* find Christ in others. Active love for others is the measure of our faith and our commitment as his disciples. We need not look far. Those who are closest to us need our love—family, friends, classmates. The lonely, the misunderstood and the mistreated all need us to pay attention to them. The poor, the physically or mentally handicapped, the aged wait for our care. Victims of prejudice are all around us. Our Lord wants us to see him in all these people and to go out of our way to love them, to meet their needs, to give them our friendship.

. *activity* .

Mohandas K. Gandhi once said, "There are so many hungry people in the world that God cannot appear to them except in the form of bread." Discuss what this means for the Christian who derives nourishment from the Lord's bread, the Eucharist.

Perhaps your class could fast for a day and donate the proceeds to a hunger center. Take up the challenge of being Christ for others by responding to the "least of these."

Conclusion: Who Do *You* Say I Am?

We began this book by looking at Jesus' timeless question, "Who do *you* say that I am?" Perhaps you are in a better position now to answer that question. You have read about our Lord, reflected on his meaning and examined what Catholics believe about him. As a searching, questioning young person, your study of and life with Jesus has just begun. There is so much more to know about Jesus. St. John told us this when he ended his gospel this way:

> There was much else that Jesus did; if it were written down in detail, I do not suppose the world itself would hold all the books that would be written   (Jn 21:25).

Perhaps you can dedicate yourself to making a lifelong study of Jesus. He lived the most fascinating of all lives. Reading and studying about Jesus is important, but more important yet is to *know* Jesus Christ *personally*.

To know Jesus as your best friend is life's greatest joy and most important task. He is the source of true happiness. How can you get closer to Jesus? How can you grow in friendship with him? Here are some questions to help you say yes to him. Jesus himself asks you:

- Do you accept me as God's Son, your savior, a friend who loves you beyond what you can imagine?
- Do you want to spend time talking to me in prayer, listening to my word in scripture, simply enjoying the love I have for you?

- Are you willing to express your sorrow when you sin, ask for my abundant forgiveness, right your wrongs and try to live as my brother or sister?

- Will you regularly receive me in the Eucharist, recognize me in your fellow Christians and look to me for guidance through my church and the leaders I have appointed to instruct you?

- Will you try to imitate me, especially by trying to serve others? Will you make an effort to help those who are especially close to me—the poor, the handicapped, the sick, the victims of injustice and the like?

- What do you think about this, my precious child? I love you! My Father loves you. And our Holy Spirit is our gift to you so that you may love, too.

▪ *journal* ▪

Write the Lord a response to the questions listed above.

▪ *summary* ▪

1. The risen Lord has chosen to be present to us through his body, the church. We are members of this body and have the life of Jesus in us. The Holy Spirit empowers us to continue his work.

2. Saints show us what a true follower of Jesus is. Mary is the model of sanctity because she showed us how to be faithful to God throughout our lives.

3. The Lord comes to us in the sacraments, sacred signs of his love. The Eucharist is a supreme sign of Jesus' love. He comes to us under the forms of bread and wine and challenges us to take him into the world.

4. Prayer and reading the Bible are ways to sense Jesus' love and presence. We must make time for them if we wish to grow in holiness.

5. The true Christian will recognize the face of Jesus in each person, but especially in "the least of these." We can't follow Jesus unless we love our neighbors as ourselves.

▪ *focus questions* ▪

1. If you decide to pray on a regular basis, what steps must you take to act on this decision?
2. Why must you love your enemy?
3. Explain the image of the church as the body of Christ.
4. Suppose someone asked you who Jesus is. List 10 things you would tell this person.

▪ *journal entries* ▪

1. Write a character sketch of Jesus as you see him. Include the following:

   Physical traits: height and weight; color of eyes and hair; build; sound of his voice; description of beard; his laugh and smile; his clothes; etc.

   His preferences: favorite drink and food; what he did for relaxation; his favorite kind of person; his least favorite kind of work; etc.

   His way with people: interactions with children; how he treated his friends; his way with strangers; how he treated sinners, outcasts, etc.; the kind of people he criticized; etc.

   What he would have said to you personally: What does Jesus think of you? What kind of friend would he be to you? What do you think of him?

   Add anything else you would like to this character sketch.

2. *Enriching your vocabulary.* Using a good dictionary, look up the meaning of the following words. Write the definitions in your journal.

   > abundant
   >
   > affective
   >
   > guileless

Prayer Reflection

Footprints

One night a man had a dream. He dreamed he was walking along the beach with the Lord. Across the sky flashed scenes from his life. For each scene, he noticed two sets of footprints in the sand; one belonging to him, and the other to the Lord.

When the last scene of his life flashed before him, he looked back at the footprints in the sand. He noticed that many times along the path of his life there was only one set of footprints. He also noticed that it happened at the very lowest and saddest times in his life.

This really bothered him and he questioned the Lord about it. "Lord, you said that once I decided to follow you, you'd walk with me all the way. But I have noticed that during the most troublesome times in my life, there is only one set of footprints. I don't understand why when I needed you most you would leave me."

The Lord replied, "My precious, precious child, I love you, and I would never leave you. During your times of trials and suffering, when you see only one set of footprints, it was then that I carried you."

—Author unknown

▪ *reflection* ▪

Think of three times when the Lord "carried you."

▪ *resolution* ▪

Promise the Lord that you will try to carry the sufferings of someone who comes into your life. Help Jesus carry his load.

Glossary of Selected Terms

Abba — A term of endearment from the Aramaic language meaning "daddy." Jesus used this word to teach that God is a loving Father.

Annunciation — The event in which the angel Gabriel announces to Mary that she is to be the mother of the Messiah (see Lk 1:26-38).

Apostle — One who is sent by Jesus to continue his work.

Ascension — Refers to that mystery whereby Jesus joined God in glory after his life on this earth was complete.

Blasphemy — An insult to or contempt of God, holy persons or things.

Christ — Greek translation of the Hebrew word for *messiah*; a significant title of Jesus meaning "the anointed one."

Covenant — The open-ended contract of love God made with the Israelites and with all people everywhere in the person of Jesus Christ.

Creed — A formal statement of faith. We recite the Nicene Creed at each Sunday Eucharist.

Disciple — A follower of Jesus who tries to live a Christ-centered life.

Evangelist — A person who proclaims the good news of Jesus Christ. "The four evangelists" refers to the authors of the four gospels: Matthew, Mark, Luke and John.

Gospel — Literally, "good news." Gospel refers to (1) the good news preached by Jesus; (2) the good news of salvation won for us in the person of Jesus Christ (he is the good news proclaimed by the church); (3) the four written records of the good news—the gospels of Matthew, Mark, Luke and John.

Idolatry — Worship of anyone or anything other than the true, living God. To put anything before God is a violation of the first commandment.

Incarnation — A key theological term for the dogma of the Son of God becoming human in Jesus Christ, born of the Virgin Mary. (The term literally means "taking on human flesh.")

Kerygma — The core or essential message of the gospel—Jesus Christ is Lord! An excellent example of the kerygma is found in Acts 2:14-36.

Lord — An important New Testament title that affirms that Jesus is God.

Magnificat — The beautiful hymn sung by Mary when she visited her cousin Elizabeth (Lk 1:46-55). It praises and thanks God for his great generosity in blessing Mary to be God's mother.

Miracle — A powerful sign that shows God at work in his creation. Jesus worked many miracles in his lifetime.

Parable — A short story told by Jesus with a striking, memorable comparison that teaches a religious message.

Paschal mystery — God's love and salvation revealed to us through the life, passion, death, resurrection and glorification of his Son Jesus Christ.

Pentateuch — The first five books of the Old Testament, the Torah, or Law, of the Chosen People. These books are Genesis, Exodus, Leviticus, Numbers and Deuteronomy.

Publicans — Tax collectors who were despised by the Jews of Jesus' day for cooperating with the Roman authorities. Jesus loved even this group of people, showing that he came for everyone.

Rabbi — A Jewish term meaning "teacher." It was a sign of respect, and many people of Jesus' day addressed him with this title.

Reign of God — The reign of God proclaimed by Jesus and begun in his life, death and resurrection. It refers to the process of God's reconciling and renewing all things through his Son, to the fact of his will being done on earth as it is in heaven. The process begun with Jesus' earthly ministry will be perfectly completed at the end of time.

Repentance — From the Greek word *metanoia*, it means change of mind or change of heart. A key aspect of following Jesus is to turn from our sins and embrace the way of the cross.

Resurrection — God's gift of eternal life given to humans who will receive a glorified body in union with Jesus Christ at the end of time. Through Jesus' death and resurrection all people have been saved.

Salvation — The process of healing whereby God's forgiveness, grace and loving attention are extended to us through Jesus Christ in the Holy Spirit. Salvation brings about union with God and with our fellow humans through the work of our brother and savior, Jesus Christ.

Sanhedrin — The chief ruling council in Jesus' day made up of the elders, the high priests and the scribes.

Son of Man — A title Jesus frequently used in speaking of himself. It meant two things: (1) Jesus' identification with all of humanity; (2) the righteous one who will usher in God's kingdom at the end of time (from Dn 7:13f).

Synoptic gospels — The gospels of Matthew, Mark and Luke. When we read them together, we note certain similarities in content and style.

Torah — The Law handed down to the Jewish people which they were to live in response to God's covenant with them. A good summary of the Torah is found in the Ten Commandments.

Transfiguration — The event in Jesus' life where his divine glory shone through his humanity, thus testifying to the fact of his true identity as God's Son. This event was witnessed by Peter, James and John (see, for example, Mt 17:1-8).

Virgin birth — The doctrine that holds that Jesus was conceived through the virgin Mary by the power of the Holy Spirit without the cooperation of a human father.

Word of God — A key title of Jesus that identifies him as the Second Person of the Blessed Trinity, the one through whom all things were made. As the Word of the Father, Jesus came to reveal his Father's will. He is the Way, the Truth and the Life.

Index

Shammai, 86
Shema, 92
Shepherds, the, 32
Sign, 64-65
Simeon, 37, 38
Simon Cyrene, 154
Simon the Pharisee, 136
Simon the Zealot, 61, 84
Sin, 64. *See also* Vices
Sisters of Jesus, 177-78
Solomon, 77
Son of Man: defined, 201; as a
    title of Jesus, 117, 118
Suetonius, 11
Suffering Servant, 80, 117, 118
"Surname" of Jesus, 35
Symbols, 168-69
Synagogue, the, 40
Synoptic gospels, 114; defined,
    201

Tacitus, 12
Taxes: Jesus' attitude toward, 98
Temple, the, 37, 38, 80, 85; Jesus
    as a boy in, 40-41
Temptations: of Jesus, 53-56;
    ours, 56-57
Ten Commandments, 76-77
Teresa of Avila, St., 187
Thaddeus, 61

Theodore of Mopsuestia, 172
Thomas (the apostle), 61, 158
Tiberius, 50
Titles of Jesus, 169-71
Torah, 40; defined, 201
Trajan, 12-13
Transfiguration, the, 136, 201

Vatican II, 178, 188
Vespasian, 13
Via Dolorosa, 154
Vices, 56-57
Virgin birth: defined, 201
Virginity of Mary, 177
Virtues, 57
Vocal prayers, 192

Washing of the feet, 148
Way of the Cross, 154
Women: Jesus and, 122, 138-40
Word of God: Jesus as, 123-24;
    defined, 201

Zacchaeus, 105
Zealots, 84-85
Zechariah (father of John the
    Baptist), 35,
Zechariah (the prophet), 80
Zerubbabel, 80